THE MEN OF THE
MARY ROSE

For all those unknown men of the Mary Rose
who did not die a dry death.

THE MEN OF THE

MARY ROSE

RAISING THE DEAD

A.J. STIRLAND

This book was first published in 2000 by John Wiley & Sons Ltd under the title *Raising the Dead*.

This new revised edition first published in 2005 by
Sutton Publishing Limited

Reprinted in 2013 by
The History Press
The Mill, Brimscombe Port,
Stroud, Gloucestershire, GL5 2QG
www.thehistorypress.co.uk

British Library Cataloguing in Publication Data
A catalogue record for this book is available from the British Library.

ISBN 978 0 7509 3915 7

Typeset in 12/15pt Photina.
Typesetting and origination by
Sutton Publishing Limited.
Printed and bound in Great Britain by
Marston Book Services Limited, Didcot

Contents

List of Figures and Plates

FIGURES

PLATES

23. Transchondral fractures (osteochondritis dissecans) of the distal femoral condyles at the knee (arrows).
24. Posterior hip joint (acetabular) rim fracture (arrow).
25. Pits in femoral heads, probably caused by a posterior fracture-dislocation.
26. A pair of beautifully preserved femurs with clear and prominent muscle insertions (arrows).
27. Bilateral os acromiale (arrows). FCS #7, found in the hold. He may have been a war bow man.
28. A modern longbow man a) at full draw and b) after release of the arrow. He is shooting a 'standard arrow' from a replica war bow of 54.5kg (120lb) draw weight. *Photograph by courtesy of H.M. Greenland.*
29. Simon Stanley at full draw. Note the position of the drawing arm and his leading foot. The bow is 'The Leopard', here held at 75kg (165lb) draw weight, in April, 1995. *Photograph by courtesy of Roy King.*
30. Simon Stanley 'laying his body into' a 63.5kg (140lb) bow. *By kind permission of H.D. Soar.*
31. New ridges and spurs of bone (known as *enthesophytes*) on the distal fibula of a young adult (arrows).
32. Enthesophytes on paired arm bones from a young adult (arrows).
33. Enthesophytes in the form of ridges (arrowheads), and deep impressions for the costoclavicualr ligaments (arrows).
34. Proximal half of a femur from the *Mary Rose*, showing areas of major muscle attachment (arrows and arrowhead).
35. Osteoarthritis (pitting) of the facet joints at the back of the spine (arrows).
36. Marginal osteophytes (extra, new bone around joints). In this example, the osteophytes have fused together (arrow).
37. Schmorl's nodes (pits in vetebral body surfaces: arrows). The spine from the *Mary Rose* is from a youngindividual, exemplified by the unfused epiphyses and 'billowing' of the surfaces of the bones (arrowheads).
38. Ossified spinal ligaments (central spinal ligaments turned to bone, arrows).
39. The large bronze culverin from M3, found with the skeletons of a number of men – the gun crew?
40. Modern replica bodkin arrowhead, made of steel. *By kind permission of Simon Stanley.*
41. Bilateral Perthes disease of the femoral heads. FCS #88.
42. FCS #88: the femurs and their matching hip joints. Bilateral Perthes disease.
43. An immature humerus with a loose epiphysis (right). A fully mature humerus with a fused epiphysis is shown on the left.

Introduction

by Robert Hardy

This new edition of Dr Stirland's important study reminds me of telephone conversations we had as she prepared the first edition. She would ask me where particular physical stresses were likely to result from shooting heavy longbows; I would answer from my own and others' experience; she would ring to say that skeletal examination confirmed the visible results of those strains known to occur in shooting.

This book is a model of how the various contributions of archaeological, historical, medical and practical research can be brought together to deepen and extend understanding of the past, in this case the whole tragic story of the loss of a Tudor warship, of great fame in its own day, and even wider fame today. Every aspect of the sinking and finally the raising of the *Mary Rose* ship, its crew and its contents is carefully detailed by Dr Stirland, and questions posed and answered. She studied the poor remains of many of those who drowned with the ship, and her conclusions bring back to us from the murk of the Solent the seamen and soldiers aboard that day in 1545, in a way that even their possessions, their weapons and their clothing to be seen in the Mary Rose Museum in Portsmouth Dockyard, cannot. Her studies reveal the exertions on board, their physical types and appearances, and the degree to which they were both very like us, and how they and the demands on their bodies differed from ours.

This is an essential work for all who study the history of naval warfare, the story of medieval and Tudor military archery, indeed the history of mankind itself.

Robert Hardy
Fellow of the Society of Antiquaries
Consultant and Trustee of the Mary Rose Trust.

Acknowledgements

A project of this size needs impetus, enthusiasm and boundless support. I am indebted to many people for providing aspects of all these at various times over the last few years. I am profoundly grateful to the Mary Rose Trust for providing the initial impetus when they invited me to record and analyse the human skeletal remains from the *Mary Rose* and, in 1985, to furnish them with a report on my work. I owe special thanks to Dr. Margaret Rule for having enough strength of character and confidence in my work to fight for the skeletal material to be kept so that my researches could continue. I owe a further debt of gratitude to Professor Don Brothwell for supporting me in these continuing research efforts. This involved extensive library work at times, some of it of a fairly obscure nature, and both the Reference Library in Northampton and the town library in Towcester provided me with a great deal of support and encouragement for which I am most grateful. For invaluable help with the initial sorting and recording of the skeletons, I thank Dr. Jacqui Bowman, Christine Osborne and Sally Parker. I was also enormously encouraged by the many people to whom I have lectured about the crew of the *Mary Rose*, both here and in the United States. There has been great interest expressed both in the ship and her crew wherever I have talked about them, whether in schools or to different groups of adults.

As far as writing this book is concerned, many friends, colleagues and other specialists have contributed ideas which have helped me. For references, copies of manuscripts and other support I would like to thank the Naval History and the General Lending Libraries in Plymouth and the West Country Studies Library and the Reference Library and Record Office in Exeter. My thanks also go to Brian Ayers, Bruce Bailey, Nick Braddock, John Coates, Stephen Fisher, Dr. David Hutchinson, Ian Murray, Dr. D. J. Ortner, Clive Powell, Dr. Carole Rawcliffe, Shire Publications and Dr. Christopher Whittaker. Lee Simpson took the photograph for Plate 15 while Hugh Soar generously provided the pictures of modern longbow men. Dr. Jennifer

Wakely took the SEM pictures used in Plates 12 and 13. I am most grateful to them all. Dr. Lynne Bell has been very generous in providing me with the results of her research, and Jenny Coy and Frank Green with the information on the victuals from the ship.

The first edition of this book would never have been written had it not been for the gentle persuasion of Helen Bailey of John Wiley and Sons, and I am grateful both to her and to Wiley for its publication. Susan Murphy and Dr. Tony Waldron read the manuscript at every stage. I am thankful to them both for all their helpful encouragement. My thanks also to N.A.M. Rodger for invaluable initial advice on the historical aspects of the naval research and to William Stanton for many interesting and useful discussions on sailing and the sea. Robert Hardy has given me much advice about longbow archery and Simon Stanley provided me with a clear insight into the workings and use of the war bow, as well as with one of his own arrows. I am indebted to them both. I also owe an enormous debt of gratitude to two individuals at the Mary Rose Trust – Andrew Elkerton and Alexzandra Hildred. In particular, Andrew has been unstintingly generous and good-natured with his time in answering my many queries and in allowing me to use materials from the Trust in this book. I owe special thanks to Dr. Julie Gardiner, without whose support and generosity in providing new illustrations this book would have been much more difficult to produce.

Above all, my thanks go to my husband Derek, who has not only read every word several times, but has provided me with some illustrations. His support of my work and of me has never faltered throughout this whole project, and both editions of this book.

Ann Stirland
August 2004

Preface

By defeating Richard Plantagenet at the Battle of Market Bosworth in August 1485, Henry Tudor gained the crown of England, becoming Henry VII, and founded a new dynasty. Thus ended the civil wars between the feuding houses of York and Lancaster, which had at times involved considerable portions of the general population. This Bright New Age was certainly a lot more peaceful than the preceding forty years or so had been, for Henry Tudor was a cautious and parsimonious king who garnered his fortune and stabilised his base. At his death, Henry's crown and considerable fortune passed to his second son, Henry VIII, a very different man from his father. This book covers the life and death of one of Henry VIII's Great Ships, the *Mary Rose* and of the men who sailed, and died, in her.

It is difficult from the perspective of the twenty-first century to visualise what it must have been like to serve in one of the King or Queen's ships during the sixteenth century. We suffer from a mixture of romanticism and horror when thinking of the past, and both reactions can be inappropriate. As in other aspects of archaeology, we tend to impose modern values and concepts on the past when considering the remains of its inhabitants, forgetting that things were very different. In 1545 we would probably have difficulty in even making ourselves understood, should we happen to arrive in Portsmouth by time machine on a certain July morning, to say nothing of how we would appear. It is also important to understand that, in any consideration of this period, there is a problem with records, which are intermittent in their survival and variable in their quality. This will be dealt with in more detail in later chapters, but the difficulty with records applies both to dates and to 'facts', which do not always tally from one author to another. I have, therefore, given as much information and as many sources as I have been able to find in all the chapter notes. I hope the reader will forgive any omissions.

ONE

Sinking and Raising:
July 1545 and October 1982

THE SINKING

England in 1544: Henry the VIII has been on the throne since 1509. From a most promising beginning as an intelligent, handsome, accomplished and poetic eighteen year old, he has deteriorated over the years into a middle-aged, louche, despotic and irresponsible monarch of unsavoury habits. He has also persistently squandered the considerable wealth left to him by his father, Henry VII, bankrupting the country. By punitive taxation and the suppression and sale of the monasteries a few years ago, he has temporarily re-filled his coffers. Why does the king require such a constant supply of money? There are two main reasons: firstly, to finance his extravagant life-style and, secondly, to wage his wars.

From the time he came to the throne, Henry VIII has been determined to try to revive the fortunes of England in France by regaining all the lands won by Edward III and Henry V and subsequently lost by succeeding kings. In this early part of the 16th century, Western Europe is dominated by France on the one hand and by the Holy Roman Empire, which rules most of Germany, the Low Countries and Italy, on the other. Henry has chosen to fight France because of its proximity and his own claims to the French throne, and has allied himself with France's enemies.

The first of Henry's French wars was that of 1512–1513, and now there is the present campaign, which seems set to continue. Throughout his reign, the two major enemies of England have been Scotland and France, who have formed an alliance, and there have been persistent problems for the king with both. In order to try and destroy this alliance His Majesty had agreed to a joint invasion of France with Charles V, the Holy Roman Emperor. The Emperor, however, has now made his own separate peace with the French, leaving the English king to fight the war alone. From the English point of view, the best result of this first year has been the successful siege and naval blockade of Boulogne between July and September, but this is having costly results for the navy since, after its capture, Boulogne has had to be supplied by the English. This is always a tricky operation, both in terms of French attack (since the English enclave is surrounded by the enemy) and the weather in the 'Narrow Seas' (the English Channel) which is unpredictable [1].

It is now 1545 and the campaign continues. Francis I, King of France, has gathered together a large fleet during the early part of the year and, by June, this is moored at the various ports on the Seine estuary, under the command of Claude d'Annebault, Admiral of France. Estimates of the size of the fleet vary between 123 and 300 vessels of which a number are

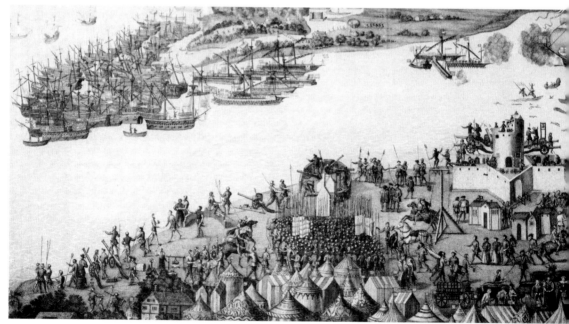

Figure 1. The Cowdray Engraving of the Spithead engagement on 19th July, 1545.
© The Society of Antiquaries of London.

sailing warships of different kinds[2]. The French intention seems to be to try to recapture Boulogne but, because the army does not appear to be ready, Francis has decided instead to attack England directly. The fleet sails on the 12th of July and, on the 16th, arrives in the Solent[3]. Meanwhile the English, aware of French intentions, have been making what preparations they can, with full-scale mobilization between February and April, so that by early June Lord Lisle (the Lord Admiral) has 160 ships and 12,000 men at sea[4]. Clearly, there is going to be a naval battle, with the French in the Solent and the English fleet in Portsmouth harbour, trapped by adverse winds.

It is the morning of Sunday, the 19th of July, and D'Annebault's navy is advancing up the Solent towards Spit Sand in three squadrons, with 26 galleys in front firing their single guns. There is little wind and the only English vessels that can engage the French at this stage are a small number of galleys, galleases and rowbarges[5]. Now, the wind has got up and the main English fleet is able to move out of Portsmouth harbour and into the Solent to engage the main French fleet (figure 1)[6]. The French galleys retreat and the battle proper begins. The English fleet is led out of harbour by the

great ships *Henry Gràce a Dieu* and the *Mary Rose*. It is getting towards evening and the *Mary Rose* is turning on to the other tack, probably to present her broadside. But she seems to have been caught by a freak gust of wind and she is heeling to starboard, filling through her open lower gun ports and sinking. Although there are at least 415 men on board,[7], only about 30 have survived; the rest are trapped by anti-boarding netting and have drowned, including the Vice Admiral for that engagement and her commander, Sir George Carew, and her captain Roger Grenville, father of the famous Richard who, in the next reign, will distinguish himself in command of the *Revenge*. It is a major disaster for England and of great propaganda benefit to the French (see Chapter 2).

THE RAISING

The reasons for the sinking of the *Mary Rose* on a calm summer evening will be discussed later, but the public nature of this sinking, only about a mile off shore and in full view of the King, his army and what must have been many onlookers will have heightened the tragedy. Not only was she one of Henry's prize ships, she was also the vessel in which his newly-appointed Vice Admiral was sailing. Obviously, it was necessary to attempt to raise her as soon as possible, a task that was overseen by the Lord Admiral, Viscount Lisle, and the military commander Charles Brandon, Duke of Suffolk. As early as the 31st of July, Suffolk wrote to Sir William Paget that he:

"Will with speed set men to the weighing (raising) of the *Mary Rose*"[8].

On the 1st of August, Paget sent Suffolk a list of:

"things necessary for the recovery with the help of God of the *Mary Rose*"

and, in a later letter that same day he:

"Trusts that by Monday or Tuesday the *Mary Rose* shall be weighed up and saved"[9].

Plans to raise the ship progressed and it appears that the decision to use two hulks, which first would be emptied, was the King's. The hulks were the

Figure 2. Patterns of erosion and collapse of the *Mary Rose* on the seabed. Copyright ©, the Mary Rose Trust.
a). First stage: the sea pours through the open gun ports (arrows) and through the decks, taking fine silts with it. The sea, on both the port and the starboard sides of the wreck, has excavated scour pits.
b). Second stage: the exposed port side collapses into the ship and, partly, into the port scour pit.
c). Final stage: a new seabed is laid down on top of the wreck, effectively sealing it.

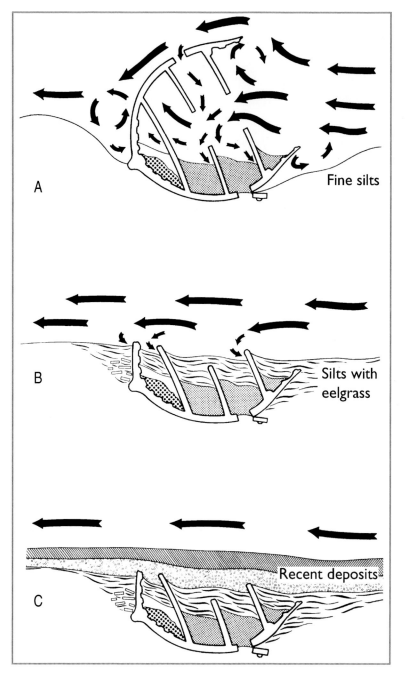

A   Fine silts

B   Silts with eelgrass

C   Recent deposits

Sampson (whose captain, Francis Finglos, had been taken "sore sick") and the *Jesus*[10]. The method was to moor these hulks on either side of the *Mary Rose*:

> "and to her masts there is tied 3 cables with other ingens (*sic*) to weigh her up, and on every side of her a hulk to set her upright"[11].

The cables would be wound tight at low tide and the empty ships would rise with the rising tide, taking the *Mary Rose* with them. The *Mary Rose*'s sails, yards and rigging had already been removed and taken ashore and it was intended that the ship should be raised on the 6th August. However, the Lord Admiral was still hoping for this to happen on the 7th of August or the following day and, on the 9th, Lisle and St. John wrote to Paget that:

> "This day the Italians who had the weighing of the Mary Roos (*sic*) signify that, by the method they have followed they cannot recover her and have broken her foremast."[12]. The Italians then asked for six more days to try and drag the vessel into "shallow ground".

All attempts to raise the *Mary Rose* immediately after she sank came to nothing. The main reasons for failure were likely to have been twofold, since salvage of ships was often undertaken with success at this time. First, the mainmast had been pulled out of its step, thus removing the main point of attachment for cables and, second, the ship sank so quickly that she became deeply embedded in the soft upper sediments of the Solent, with her keel resting on the heavy clay layer two to three metres below, thus becoming effectively stuck. Further attempts to raise the ship in the sixteenth century were abandoned and, gradually, the exposed port side became eroded, collapsing into the hull and surrounding scour pits (figure 2). Gravel, shells and other debris settled over the wreck to form a hard, compact seabed and she was forgotten. Periodically, storms would remove part of this seabed, exposing the tops of some of the timbers, which entangled the nets of local fishermen. Then, the timbers would be covered again until the next exposure.

John and Charles Deane were brothers and marine salvage engineers who devised a successful underwater breathing apparatus (figure 3). In 1836 they were invited to investigate an area of the seabed at Spithead where fishermen's lines were frequently caught. When they dived on the area, the Deanes found a large bronze demi-cannon and old timbers exposed on the seabed. A later dive yielded three more guns from the same wreck area and it

Figure 3. A contemporary painting of the Deane brothers working on the wreck of the *Royal George*, which had sunk at Spithead in 1782. Copyright © the Mary Rose Trust.

was decided, by a committee set up by the Board of Ordnance, that the wreck from which the guns had come must be that of the *Mary Rose*. During the next four years the Deanes recovered a variety of artefacts from the site, including several human skulls, and it is now clear that what they were finding came from the exposed and collapsed port side of the ship[13]. The matter might have rested there had it not been for the vision of Alexander McKee, an amateur diver and journalist, who founded Project Solent Ships in 1965 in order to search for and record wrecks in the Solent.

There are many wrecks around the coasts of Great Britain. They are in a varied state of preservation, according to the conditions of their burial and the nature of the particular seabed sediments. Project Solent Ships was intended to examine several wrecks from the sixteenth century onwards. The small group of people involved with this intermittent project included Margaret Rule as the professional archaeologist. She would eventually become the project leader in the work on the *Mary Rose*. Initially, however, the ship had to be found and this proved to be difficult, since the hull was totally buried. Eventually, in 1967, the wreck was found using a dual

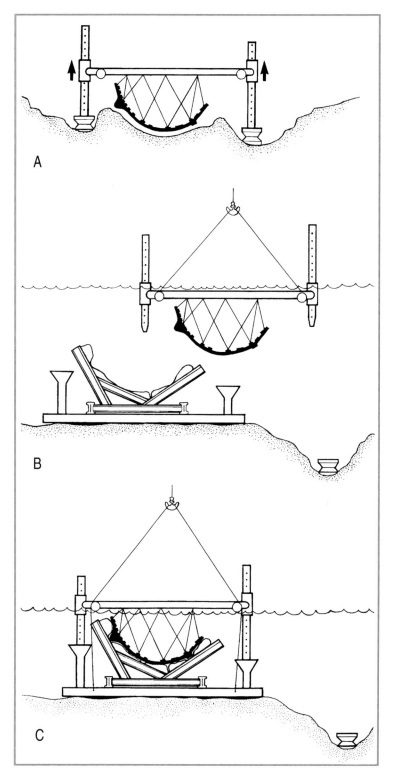

Figure 4. The raising
of the *Mary Rose*.
Copyright © the Mary
Rose Trust.
a). A frame is lowered
to the seabed and the
wreck attached to it
by steel hawsers.
b). A cradle is lowered
next to the frame.
The frame, with the
wreck, is lifted by
crane.
c). The cradle
containing the wreck
is lifted by the crane
up and on to the
barge (not shown).

channel side-scanner and sonar. The side scan showed, by use of acoustic signals, anomalies on the seabed surface and the sonar profiled the buried subsurface. An anomaly was revealed, roughly in the area where the ship later proved to be resting, below the sediments on the seabed. The wreck itself was not found by excavation until 1971, and then volunteers, with limited funds and equipment, excavated on the site until 1978. Protection of the area was afforded by the Historic Wreck Act, which was passed by Parliament in 1973. In 1978, the excavation uncovered an area at the bow of the ship which was preserved just as it had been in 1545 when it settled on the seabed, with artefacts, personal possessions and ship's stores all intact. The Mary Rose Committee, which had been formed in 1967, recognised the cultural, military and historic importance of the ship and it was decided to excavate the hull completely and attempt to recover her for conservation and permanent display[13].

The problems that the original salvors encountered in trying to lift the *Mary Rose* from the seabed were finally overcome by the use of a specially designed lifting frame. Divers drilled the empty hull and bolted steel hawsers into it[14]. The hawsers were attached to a steel frame which covered the area of the ship and which had a telescopic leg at each corner (figure 4a). A cradle, which was the same shape as the hull, was made, lined with air bags, and then lowered to the seabed at the side of the wreck (figure 4b). The intention was to lower the legs on the frame until it was stable on the bottom, winch the legs up until the wreck became unstuck, place it in the air-bag lined cradle and winch the whole lot up to the surface (figure 4c). At the surface, there would be a barge on which the hull in its cradle could be placed and then the entire structure towed back into Portsmouth harbour. As is often the case the weather also played its part and, on the proposed day of lifting, it was appalling. However, using the above techniques, the *Mary Rose* was successfully lifted from the seabed on October the 11th, 1982, and broke the surface once again. Modern technology had succeeded where the sixteenth century Italian salvage experts could not.

NOTES

1. See, among others, Rodger, for details of this campaign.
2. Rodger says there were 150 ships and 25 galleys (p. 183), while Loades suggests between 50 and 150 (p. 131). Other estimates include 200 sail and 26 galleys. Whatever the true numbers, it was obviously a large and ominous fleet.

3. See Loades, p131.

4. According to Loades. Again, estimates vary. Rodger states that Lisle was heavily outnumbered and only had about 80 ships; Oppenheim states that there were 85 vessels and 13 rowbarges. All sources suggest that the French seriously outnumbered the English.

5. Descriptions of these vessels will be found in the Glossary.

6. The 'Cowdray Engraving', one of the few sources for this battle, was an eighteenth century engraving of the scene on the 19th of July, 1545 when the *Mary Rose* sank. It was commissioned by the Society of Antiquaries from an original contemporary painting in Cowdray House, which was destroyed by fire a few years afterwards. The contemporary documentary evidence for the event is scanty but is described in Rule. Both the French and English versions of these events are further discussed by de Brossard.

7. The situation with regard to the number of men on board the ship on the day she sank is confusing, to say the least. The Anthony Roll lists the numbers as 185 soldiers, 200 mariners and 30 gunners - a total of 415. However, numerous writers have given other figures and there have been suggestions in some quarters that there were an extra 300 archers on board on the day she sank. This may be true, but there is no documentary evidence for it and, when I enquired about sources, I was told that the figure was apocryphal and had come from a relative of a drowned crew member who observed the tragedy (M. Rule, personal communication). See also Chapter 2, reference 52.

8. L and P 31 July 1545, 1325 R.O.

9. L and P 1 August 1545, 2, 3. R.O. st P.1; 796 and 798. See also Rule 1982 for the full list of the equipment needed to raise such a ship. Rule also suggests that the planned salvage of the vessel was perfectly feasible in shallow coastal waters and the method had been used many times before.

10. L and P 2 August 1545,16. R.O. st P. 1, 800 Lisle to Paget.

11. L and P 5 August 1545, 38. R.O. st P. 1, 801.

12. L and P 9 August 1545, 81. R.O.

13. See Rule for some account of all this.

14. When the hull was drilled, fresh heartwood was found to have survived 437 years of submarine burial.

TWO

The King's Ships and the Navy Royal

The Tudor navy was very much an aspect of the state and the King's ships demonstrated his power. When Henry Tudor became Henry VII he both lessened his dependence on the nobility and developed his own personal power during the course of his reign. He increased his revenues and built two large warships and an embryonic naval base at Portsmouth. His son, Henry VIII, followed many of his father's policies, increasing his direct control of much of the country by royal commissions and by the introduction of new revenue courts to handle the income from the suppression and sale of the monasteries.

Henry VIII was a tall, handsome man of great physical energy. He excelled at sports of all kinds and had a great love of life[1]. He was also interested in his new ships and the sea and sometimes acted as an amateur pilot, wearing the symbolic whistle[2]. Like earlier medieval monarchs, absolute power was vested in him and he was a bombastic and warlike king, fond of grand gestures which he could not afford. His armed ships were a status symbol and he created a whole new infrastructure of storehouses and dockyards and, in effect, a standing navy institutionalising all these innovations as a part of government[3].

It is often said that Henry VIII was the father of the Royal Navy. While he was certainly responsible for building or otherwise acquiring a large number of ships, the statement is only partly true. Henry does not seem to have had a real appreciation of the importance of naval power, at least at the beginning of his reign. His chosen course of action, however, involving war with France and her allies abroad, particularly Scotland, could only be undertaken with a reasonable naval force and so circumstances, in the form of his military ambitions, seem to have forced his hand. At the same time, conditions of land warfare in Europe were changing from their medieval forms and the navy, such as it was, was beginning to change too[4]. It has to be said that Henry does not seem to have acknowledged the importance of sea power per se. This is exemplified both by his continuing to charter his ships for civilian use, even when there was much political tension, and by his inability to develop any good naval strategies during his reign[5].

When he inherited the throne in 1509, Henry also inherited from his father a small fleet, including the two Great Ships *Sovereign* and *Regent*; the *Sovereign* was about 450 tons and the *Regent* about 600 tons. A ship's size is defined by its tonnage. Loades states:

"Tonnage was a measure of displacement, not weight, and was based upon an estimation of the number of tuns of Bordeaux wine with which a ship could be loaded."[6].

Loades also gives Prynne's formula for estimating tonnage as:

"depth of hold, multiplied by keel length, multiplied by main beam, and divided by 100"[7].

This differs a little from Coates' definition, which is:

"length of keel × breadth × depth of hold divided by 97"[8].

A confusion sometimes arises in the terminology used when describing the size of these ships, where tonnage can be expressed as a ship's 'burthen' or 'burden'. Rodger[9], defines these last terms as:

"the internal volume or cargo capacity of a ship".

Both the *Sovereign* and the *Regent* were four-masted carracks of overlapping clinker build, rather than the edge-to-edge carvel construction which was to become the norm. They appear to have been the first large, heavily armed, purpose-built warships. A programme of maintenance and building existed which had started in the previous reign with dockyards, certainly in Woolwich and Portsmouth, a reasonably active naval administration based at Portsmouth, and a Clerk of the Ships in charge of the storehouses. The first important Clerk of the King's Ships, at least in terms of the development of Tudor naval administration, was Robert Brigandyne, who served both Henry VIII and his father.

The *Sovereign* and the *Regent* were not built for any specific war or campaign but they never became redundant, being well maintained and requiring special docking. Until this time, docking for routine maintenance had taken place in mud docks on beaches but this was inadequate for such Great Ships. So, in 1496 a new dock was built at Portsmouth, together with a forge and storehouse, initially for the purpose of maintaining these two ships. It has been described as the first known dry dock in England although this is debatable. It was a new structure in the sense that it had a deep, timber-lined basin and was closed with double wooden gates; nevertheless, it was still necessary to shore up the dockhead with large quantities of stone and rubble. This rubble filled the space between the gates and, like the mud docks, had to be dug out at low tide in order that a ship could leave the dock when the tide rose. A true dry dock is a permanent fixture which ships can enter or leave on a high tide because it has gates that allow this; it does not have to be dug out at low tide every time it is used. It seems that even the dock itself was not really new but a re-build from an earlier, original form, built in 1492. The only difference from the conventional mud docks seems to have been in the timbered dock head and the inner and outer coffer dams enclosing an earth filling. It was only used for long stays and, although it had a pump to help in emptying it, pumps had been in use on ships for some time and were probably not a novelty for a dock. Discussion of this dock occurs in Kitson, Loades and Rodger and is interesting in view of the subsequent building of the *Mary Rose*. Kitson[10] considered the dock to be an innovation but Rodger states very clearly that it was neither new nor the first dry dock[11]. Loades says that excavation started:

"on the site of the later No. 1 basin on 24 June 1495"[12].

The remains of a sixteenth century ship, thought to be the *Sovereign*, were found in 1912 on the site of Woolwich power station; she was known to have been abandoned at Woolwich in 1621[13]. The *Sovereign* was rebuilt in 1509–10, soon after Henry VIII's accession, and she may have been converted at this time from clinker to carvel construction, with some additional strengthening of the hull[13]. The Woolwich ship has such a change in construction, including strengthening of the hull, which may have been required to accommodate an internal deck strong enough to support guns that were heavier than usual.

In order to further his ambitions in France and his campaigns elsewhere, the King increased his navy in several ways. He bought a number of big ships and, as his father had done, built two large ones. These were the *Peter Pomegranate* and the *Mary Rose* named, it is said, after his favourite sister, Mary Tudor. By December, 1511, Henry possessed 13 ships of his own; this represented the largest royal fleet since the time of Henry V. By the end of the reign, there were more than 80 ships in the royal fleet. Five further ships were definitely built for him during 1512, three more were probably built and six more were bought. These varied from 80 to 700 tons and three were described as galleys. Rodger defines a galley as:

"A type of warship propelled primarily by oars"[14].

Of Mediterranean origin, they were much lighter and easier to manoeuvre than the large sailing warships. The French used them to great effect and inflicted considerable damage at close range, especially on the English.

All this development was to enable Henry to wage war by both land and sea and he did not view his ships merely as troop transporters[15], as they had been in the past. Probably the largest and most famous of the King's ships was the *Henry Grace à Dieu*, often known as the *Great Harry*. She was launched in February or March of 1513.

THE *MARY ROSE*

The keel of the *Mary Rose* was laid in 1509, although whether this occurred before of after the death of Henry VII in the April of that year is unclear, according to Loades[16]. This is an interesting point since the possibility of the *Mary Rose* being started during Henry VII's reign implies both that he was intending to increase his fleet and that there was, indeed, continuity of intention between the two reigns. The confusion about when her keel was laid is due to the medieval practice of dating documents according to the Regnal Year, which was the actual year of the ruling monarch's reign. Thus, since

Henry VII died on 21 April, 1509, Henry VIII's regnal year was from 22 April to the 21 April, spanning parts of two calendar years. So, if the *Mary Rose's* keel was laid in March 1509, it would be the year 24 Henry VII, but if it was laid on 22 April or later in 1509, it would be the year 1 Henry VIII. This has some relevance when considering documents[17].

She appears to have been built during 1510:

"Warrant directed, 29 January 1510, to John Dawtrey for the 'new making' of the *Mary Rose* and *Peter Pomegranate*".[18]

This date also appears in Loades, who mentions a letter from Brigandyne to Richard Polshide:

"another customer of Southampton, about money received for the repair of the *Sovereign* and the new making of the *Mary Rose* and the *Peter Pomegranate* – the first time those famous ships appear in the records".[19]

Clearly, the Brigandyne letter must have been written in 1510, since the previous item,(vii), a letter to Dawtrey and Polshide about the repair of the *Sovereign*, is dated "28 Oct. 1 Hen.VIII" that is, 1509. Therefore, the next letter, dated 9 June, must be 1510, because the Regnal Year began on 22 April (see above).

After building she was towed, together with the *Peter Pomegranate*, round to the Thames to be fitted-out, probably at Woolwich[20]. The ship seems to have been finished in time for the first French war of 1512–1514 and was probably commissioned at the beginning of 1512. It has been suggested that the *Mary Rose* was built in the 'new' Portsmouth dock discussed above, along with the *Peter Pomegranate*[21]. However, since no records of these events survive, it is difficult to know if this is the case. The earliest mention of the *Mary Rose* by name is in the letter of 1510, and it seems that she was built, finished and commissioned within two to three years.

The only 'contemporary' representation of the ship comes from the Anthony Roll. In 1546, Anthony compiled a list of all the King's ships and he included the *Mary Rose*, although she had sunk the previous year. The illustration shows the ship as she was after her major re-build in 1536 (figure 5) and is a stylised, although carefully detailed, sixteenth century representation. The archaeological evidence from the surviving hull structure suggests a rather different image of a ship that may have been more sea-worthy (figure 6). Whichever picture we accept, the basic structure of the ship remains the same and, clearly, she was purpose-built as a warship. Previous vessels had been adapted when necessary for war by adding fore and aft fighting castles on to an existing structure.

CONSTRUCTION

The *Mary Rose* was a four-masted carrack with four decks. Some sources quote her original burthen as 500 tons[22, 23] while others state she was 400 tons, uprated to 700 tons after her major refit[24]. When she sank, the *Mary Rose* was an old ship, having been on active service for more than thirty years. She was refurbished several times during her long life. Rodger states she was

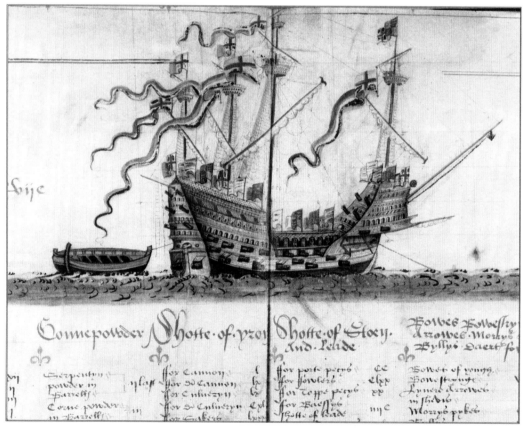

Figure 5. The Anthony Roll picture of the *Mary Rose*. By kind permission of the Pepys Library, Magdalen College, Cambridge.

rebuilt twice – in 1527 and 1536[25] – and, as well as these rebuilds, Loades also mentions that she was caulked in August 1518[26]. Apart from an elm keel, she was built almost entirely of oak and the construction is interesting, as explained below[27].

There are two main techniques for constructing ships' hulls of wood:

1. Clinker (or clench) construction, where the hull is built up from the keel with overlapping planks, and frames are inserted later for strength.
2. Carvel construction, where the frame of the ship is built first and then clad with edge-to-edge planking.

Clinker construction is the older of the two techniques and has one major disadvantage for a warship – it is impossible to cut gun ports through the hull and build lids for them which fit securely enough to be fully waterproof. Therefore, such gun ports cannot be made below, or close to, the water line.

Figure 6. A modern representation of the *Mary Rose*, based on archaeological evidence from the surviving hull structures. © The Mary Rose Trust.

Hinged gun-port lids do not seem to have been used before the sixteenth century[28], and both Anthony's illustration and the modern reconstruction show some gun ports with lids and some without. It has been suggested that the *Mary Rose* was originally clinker built and:

"had been designed with only two gunports on each side on her lower deck"[29].

However, it is also suggested that she was the first ship:

"known to have been designed to carry heavy guns on a gun deck above the orlop"[30].

The archaeological evidence from the hull shows a ship that has a carvel-constructed hull and a castle deck that is clinker built. There are also hinged gun-port lids on the main gun deck in the carvel-built hull, and unlidded ports on the upper and castle decks[31].

The surviving ship consists of a bow-to-stern section through the centre, with the whole port side and the bow (fore) castle missing, but including the partly surviving stern (after) castle, and the hold. Starting at the keel, there is the hold, containing ballast, stores and the galley or galleys. Two skeletons were found in the hold, with remnants of straw close by. It has been suggested that these individuals may have been either sick or wounded[32] and they will be discussed later. Above the hold is the orlop deck, which contained stores, equipment and hand weapons such as longbows, and above this is the main deck which housed large guns and three surviving cabins – probably those of the barber surgeon, the pilot and the carpenter. The upper deck contained hand weapons and guns and, in practice, would have been the area where the archers stood behind removable blinds in order to fire on the enemy. The blinds which protected them were made from poplar. On the highest deck – the castle – were more guns[33]. The fore and main masts were square rigged and the mizzen and bonaventure masts were lateen [triangular] rigged. The exposed decks were covered with a frame of anti-boarding netting which can be clearly seen on both the upper deck and the aftercastle in the Anthony drawing (figure 5). This served the purpose of keeping the enemy off when two fighting ships hove to and grappled during battle. In this instance, probably because she sank so quickly, the netting trapped the majority of the men on board so that of the 415 or so probably present on that day, only about three dozen survived; the rest were drowned. Those that survived were probably in the fighting tops. These were platforms, similar to a 'crow's nest', built at the top of the masts and probably used primarily by archers to shoot at the enemy from a good height. The Cowdray engraving clearly shows someone jumping from one of these tops as the ship sinks (figure 1).

ARMAMENT

The three most heavily armed warships in Henry VIII's fleet in 1540 were the *Great Harry*, the *Great Galley* and the *Mary Rose*. The efficient arming of a warship while still maintaining her ability to keep afloat had always been a problem, compounded by the traditional method of clinker construction. Whether she was the *Sovereign* or not, it seems that the Woolwich ship had been rebuilt at some point, possibly to accommodate a gun deck. There is evidence of a change to carvel construction, with the addition of strengthening frames and riders to the hull[34]. Apart from the development of gun decks, the other major innovation in the big warships was the adoption of the flat transom stern and the cutting in to this stern of a couple of gun ports, low down near the water line and at either side of the rudder. This area became known as the gunroom and a couple of long heavy guns, known as 'stern chasers', were mounted here (figure 5). These may have been the first really large guns to be used in sailing warships. Such guns were useful to bombard the shore and to protect the stern from attack by galleys[35].

Galleys were the scourge of the heavier sailing warships. They were fast, manoeuvrable and, most importantly, fired forwards while the warships could only fire broadside or astern. A galley fleet could, and did, attack over a wide range with heavy guns. The sailing ships, however, could only respond with small arms fire, at least from a distance, since the heavy armament that the big ships carried could only be fired at short range. The galleys used their advantage in firepower to great effect. The Cowdray engraving of the Spithead action clearly shows this tactic. Three French galleys have engaged the *Great Harry* in the front of the fleet, while most of the rest of the ships have not been able even to raise sail (figure 1). Even when the sailing ships had been adapted with proper gun decks and could mount heavier artillery, they were still only able to fire broadside. In some vessels, however, the guns could be turned to fire in a more forward or aft direction, and this was an improvement. For example, the Cowdray engraving also shows the *Great Harry* firing on the French galleys with a port side gun that has been turned as far forward as possible. Nevertheless, in inshore waters, such as those in this Spithead battle, the galleys were lethal.

In the early part of the reign, the big guns that were taken to sea were almost always breech-loaders, built up like a barrel with iron staves, bound by iron hoops shrunk on to them and mounted on wheels[36]. Such guns had detachable breech chambers and could be re-loaded without moving the gun. Some of them were extremely large, sometimes at least twenty feet long, and weighing as much as five tons, but their firing range was very short. The development of carvel construction, hull strengthening and gun decks with lidded gun ports low down near the water line, enabled heavy guns to be carried on the sailing warships. A further innovation was the introduction of cast bronze or wrought iron muzzle-loading heavy guns, which were loaded from the front. They could fire heavier charges than the earlier guns and had a longer range. This led to the adoption of sliding carriages, which could absorb the shock of the recoil. Both types of gun will be discussed further in Chapter 8. The adoption of sliding gun carriages seems to have occurred first on Mediterranean galleys[37], and this innovation by the galleys posed real problems of survival for the cumbersome, broadside-firing warships. Attempts were made to overcome the problems of broadside firing by mounting a couple of heavy guns high up on the first stage of the after castle of the warships. These were designed to fire forward in arcs, clearing the forecastle on either side. Although they were forward-firing guns, however, there was still a large 'blind spot' straight ahead in which they could not reach the smaller galleys – they were mounted too high. Only the guns in the gunroom, firing astern, could do this.

Nine riders were added to brace the hull of the *Mary Rose*, probably during her final re-build in 1536. These were cut to fit over the keelson and the fore-and-aft stringers. Wooden braces were also fitted to the ship, running through the edge of the orlop deck and into the hold[38]. This strengthening of the hull was probably to support heavy guns on a gun deck. She may have had some kind of a gun deck earlier, as Loades suggests, but this increased strength will have enabled her to carry much heavier armament. She also had at least one forward-firing gun mounted on the after castle[39] and, if the Anthony illustration is correct, four guns mounted on the forecastle, firing aft. There appear to have been a further six guns high on the stern, on the after castle and above the gunroom, also firing aft (figure 5). These guns will all have been fired through gun ports without lids, cut into the clinker planking of the castles. It is interesting that the modern reconstruction, based on the archaeological evidence from the excavations, shows her with four forward-firing guns, two on the after castle and two on the forecastle (figure 6).

When she sank in 1545 the *Mary Rose* was carrying a mixed armament comprising both wrought iron breech-loaders and cast bronze muzzle-loaders. This is clear from the results of the excavation[40] and also from the guns brought up by the Deane brothers[41]. The excavation of the hull produced guns:

". . . found in situ on the starboard side of the ship; seven on the main deck, three on the upper deck, four on the castle deck and one on the upper deck in the after castle. . . ."[42].

This is, of course, only the starboard half of the ship and the guns from the port side, the missing forecastle and the rest of the after castle are not there. The Deanes may have brought up some of these.

A list of ships' armaments of 1540 gives the *Mary Rose* a total of 81 guns after her refit, including eight heavy guns (demi-culverin and others)[43]. However, Oppenheim speaks of the *Mary Rose* having:

"79 guns (besides six in her tops), of which 33 were serpentines, 26 stone guns, and 10 murderers, but she also had five brass curtalls and five brass falcons."[44]

She is listed in the Anthony Roll as having 91 guns. Whichever way we look at it, it is clear that the *Mary Rose* was heavily armed and had been brought by rebuilding to a state-of-the-art ship. However, heavy armament in the form of big guns was not the only ordnance the ship was carrying when she sank.

A state paper of July 1513 details weapons other than heavy guns carried on the King's ships at the time of the invasion of France. The *Mary Rose* is listed as having, among other things:

"Bows = 350; Bowstrings = 700; Sheaves of arrows = 700; Bills = 300 (billhooks); Morrispikes = 300; Stakes = 200 (footnote = to defend archers in the field); Harness = 220 (armour)"[45].

Apart from the bills and morrispikes for hand-to-hand fighting, there was obviously a considerable amount of archery equipment aboard, at least in 1513. The English archer had been a most successful fighting unit during the medieval period, dominating France and producing notable victories at Crécy [1346] and Agincourt [1415]. His weapon was a yew longbow and it was used to great effect as a saturation weapon, arrows being fired simultaneously by archers in line abreast into the air to achieve maximum penetration[46]. By the sixteenth century, the longbow was coming to the end of its active life as a weapon of war, as the development of hand guns and the small, portable arquebus gradually overtook it. It was still in use in 1545, however, and much archery equipment was recovered from the wreck, including 172 longbows, 138 of which were complete, and more than 3,500 arrows in boxes and sheaves. Also recovered were leather discs in which 24 arrows could be held and leather arm guards (bracers) designed to protect the bow arm of the archer when the string recoiled after shooting[47]. The bows were made from a single piece of yew and the bow staves were imported from Poland and Switzerland among other places (see Chapter 8). Indeed, Henry had to import nearly everything he needed for his wars against France and Scotland and this exhausted the national resources to an alarming degree as his capital was drained away[48].

It has been suggested that a gun crew on the *Mary Rose* consisted of about six men including an archer to cover the open gun port while the gun was hauled back into the gun deck for refuelling[32], (see also Chapter 8). It is also suggested that longbow men lined the upper deck amidships and fired abreast on the enemy from behind the removable poplar blinds. Others would have been in the fighting tops, picking off targets on enemy ships. It is possible that there was a group of 'special' or 'elite' archers on board when she sank, since some elaborately decorated bracers were found during the excavation, including at least one embellished with a pomegranate, the personal symbol of Catherine of Aragon. Evidence from the human skeletal remains supports this idea and suggests that some of these men may have been specialist archers (see Chapter 8).

WHY DID THE *MARY ROSE* SINK?

The *Mary Rose* had been praised for both her handling qualities and her speed, at least early in her life:

"Sir, sche is the noblest shipp of sayle [of any] gret ship, at this hour, that I trow be in Christendom"[49].

Her sinking must have been a great shock to those who witnessed it, particularly as the Vice Admiral, Sir George Carew, was on board. There are various schools of thought as to its cause.

When she sank, the *Mary Rose* heeled over and landed on her starboard side, coming to rest at an angle of 60° from the vertical[50]. It appears that she came to grief either attempting to raise sail or turning to present her broadside to the French ships. The French claimed that they had sunk her with gunfire from their galleys, and this seemed possible, given the ability of these galleys to do a great deal of damage, as we have seen. Martin du Bellay made these claims in his memoirs and they appear in several sources[51]. So, the archaeologists who excavated the wreck were keen to see whether there was evidence from examination of the hull of any enemy action that might have sunk her. No such evidence was found by excavation. Furthermore, there is a reasonable suspicion that du Bellay was indulging in special pleading in his claims that the French had sunk her. An article by de Brossard argues this very strongly, making the point that the du Bellays were very close to the French king and it was in their interests to present the sinking of the *Mary Rose* as a success for the French galleys[52]. What other event might have caused the sinking?

John Hooker, writing after 1575, gives an account of the sinking. Hooker was the contemporary biographer of Sir Peter Carew, Sir George's brother[53]. In this account of the sinking Sir Peter says that Sir George ordered the sails of the *Mary Rose* to be hoist and she began immediately to heel. Sir Gawain Carew, uncle of Peter and George, passed by the ship and asked his nephew, George:

". . . how he did, who answered he had the sort of knaves whom he could not rule . . ."[53].

This comment has been taken by many authors to indicate that there was insubordination among the crew, which contributed to the sinking.

However, James Watt suggests that there is a strong possibility that the Mary Rose may have been struck by an epidemic of dysentery and that the 'knaves' were actually sick and too debilitated to respond to orders[54].

Another suggestion is that the *Mary Rose* had become, with age, critically unstable. Coates states that:

"in commission, all ships tend to increase in weight. They 'grow'!"[8].

Such growth is a function of the density of a ship's population and equipment, including the many personal objects that find their way on board[8]. It is suggested that the *Mary Rose*'s accumulation of weight over time, coupled with overloading, led to her sinking[8]. Another author takes this a little further, suggesting that the unruly seamen may have realised that the ship was unstable and, in effect, a death trap[55] thus leading, understandably, to some insubordination.

The archaeological evidence does not support the argument that the *Mary Rose* was sunk in battle by the French galleys. The best argument, suggested by the archaeologists and described by Rodger is that:

"Late in the day the *Mary Rose*, going about on to the other tack, was caught by a flaw of wind, filled through her open gunports, and sank with the loss of almost all on board"[56].

There is some support for this idea. Apparently, while wind may often be absent in the morning it can appear after lunch and increase during the rest of the day, sometimes up to a force seven by evening. Such a wind only occurs on a hot summer's day, and is caused by convection, the warmed air rising over the land as the day wears on and pulling cooler air in from the sea, giving rise to an on-shore wind[57]. It is worth remembering that the summer of 1545 was very hot[58]. Thus, we have a ship that was in all probability critically unstable, caught in an ever-increasing wind and executing a clumsy manoeuvre. The rest, as they say, is history.

NOTES

1. Fraser, pp. 53–56.
2. Opp., p. 48.
3. A more detailed discussion of this will be found in Loades' Introduction.
4. Opp., p. 47.
5. Rodger makes this point on a number of occasions and his argument is persuasive. See, in particular, chapter 13.

6. Loades, p. 12 – footnote. A 'tun' was a large cask for beer or wine with a capacity of 252 wine gallons. 'To lade' was to put cargo on board a ship.
7. MM, 54, 1968: 123.
8. *The Naval Architect*, June 1985.
9. Rodger, p. 591.
10. MM, 33, 1947: pp. 256-257.
11. Rodger, p. 71.
12. Loades, p. 41.
13. See Rule, pp. 22–23 for a description and illustrations of this ship; Rodger, p. 204 mentions the strengthening of the hull.
14. Rodger, p. 596 .
15. Loades, p. 57. A list of all the ships built or acquired during the reign is in Oppenheim – p. 49 *et seq.*
16. Loades p. 49.
17. Richardson, p. 59.
18. Spont, footnote, p. 4.
19. Loades p 55.
20. L and P, Vol 1, Pt. 2, p 1495 *et seq.* 3608: John Daunce's accounts: "1511 July 29, John Daunce paid, by the King's command, to Robert Brigandyne, clerk of the King's ships, for conveyance of two new ships, the *Mary Rose* and the *Peter Granade (sic)* from Portsmouth to the Thames 120 l. [l = £1]
    September 9, for expenses of the two new ships now at Thames 30 l.
    September 24, for expenses of the two new ships lying in the Thames 50 l." etc.
21. See MRT 3, p. 3.
22. Opp., p. 49.
23. Spont, p. xiv.
24. MRT 3, p. 4.
25. Rodger, p. 207.
26. Loades, p. 69.
27. The construction of the ship is comprehensively dealt with in MRT 3, 1997, p. 13 *et seq.*
28. G. F. Howard, 1981: Gun-Port Lids.
29. Loades, p. 67.
30. *Op cit.*, p. 49.
31. MRT 3, p. 15.
32. Margaret Rule, personal communication, 1984.
33. See MRT 3, pp. 19 and 25 for clear diagrams and photographs of all these features.
34. Rodger p. 204.
35. Rodger has a clear and fascinating discussion on the development of warship design and armament pp. 204–6.
36. MRT, 3 p. 22 has a drawing of one of these guns recovered from the wreck.
37. Rodger p. 208.

38. MRT, 3 p. 13 has a description of the ship and a drawing of some of the details of her construction.
39. *Op cit.*, p. 15 shows one of the forward-firing guns up in the aftercastle, as found on excavation.
40. Rule, p. 165.
41. *Op cit.*, p. 43.
42. MRT, 3 p 14.
43. Anderson, Notes MM, 6, p 281.
44. Opp. p. 55.
45. *Op cit.*, p. 56.
46. The technique was demonstrated to great effect in the Olivier film version of 'Henry V'.
47. MRT, 3 p. 26.
48. Rodger, p. 189.
49. Letter from Sir Edward Howard to Henry VIII, written aboard the *Mary Rose* and dated 22 March, 1513. L & P, Vol. 1, Part 1. 1698 [Calig D VI 101 BM Ellis 25 I 213].
50. Rule, p. 44.
51. M. de Brossard, p 387, Entick, p 158 and Rule, p. 36–38, discuss the claims.
52. M. de Brossard *op cit.*
53. Published by Sir T. Philips as 'The Life of Sir Peter Carew of Mohun Ottery, co. Devon' in *Archaeologia* Vol. 28, Pt.I, 1839, pp. 109–11. In this same extract, Sir Peter is reported to have said that the "sayde Mary Roose, thus heelinge more and more, was drowned, with 700 men wiche were in here" (see my Chapter 1, reference 7). Since he also goes on to say that "he had in the shipp a hundrith maryners", however, the report may not be very accurate. Neither figure tallies with the Anthony Roll. Furthermore Hollinshed, first published in 1577, speaks of "foure hundreth souldioures" on board, a figure much closer to the Anthony Roll total (1577, Vol ii, p. 1062, Horsey).
54. Watt *MM*, 69, p. 17.
55. Barker, *MM*, 78, p. 439.
56. Rodger, p. 183.
57. William Stanton, personal communication, 1999.
58. Rodger, p. 234.

THREE

Early Sixteenth Century England: the Social Fabric

THE GENERAL POPULATION

Although the sixteenth century represents the beginnings of the Early Modern Age and the end of the Middle Ages, the basic form of society was still a residual feudalism. In 1500 the fundamental unit of landownership was the manor, and the lord of the manor still retained his demesne – land for his own use plus the accompanying tenancies. He would also own pasture, woodland and fisheries and the seigniorial rights to various activities, such as the holding of courts, each of which brought in profit[1]. Probably less than half the manors had a permanently resident lord, his interests being represented by a steward or seneschal. Nevertheless the lord, or his steward, had a very important personal relationship with each of his tenants, since the success of the system depended on their mutual interdependence[2].

By this period, there was much more owner-occupation of land then had been the case earlier. Nevertheless, the idea of absolute ownership of land by any single individual was impossible. All land was ultimately the property of the crown, either directly or through tenure to a superior lord. Some lords held honours or baronies, which often included castles and their accompanying settlements, directly from the crown.

Tenure and its relationships with the lord or lords was a complicated business. Tenants could fall into several categories. They could be freeholders, paying a small, fixed rent and enjoying legal security. Within this was some land held by 'socage' where there were some fixed services but not the usual obligation of military service. All freeholding could be disposed of, or inherited, without any restriction. Copyholders were the successors of medieval villeins (unfree tenants). They could show written evidence of their tenancy in the manorial court rolls. Tenancies were either virtually freehold or at the lord's disposal, new tenants paying entry fines. After the earlier depopulation of the Black Death and the resulting shortage of labour, many of these copyholdings were purchased from the lords. Leasehold was based on freely negotiated contracts between two parties and recorded in indentures. The leases could be for lives, that is for one or more living people, or for years. The common law courts protected the leases for lives.

The individuals with the most secure tenures were wealthy farmers occupying large farms: the yeomen. They regarded themselves, and were widely accepted, as men of a higher status than their neighbours[3]. They formed a small farming aristocracy, many of whose sons went to Oxford or Cambridge and then into the church. Thus, society was structured, from the top downward, into groups consisting of: the nobility, the gentry, burgesses and leading citizens, and yeomen, followed by poor husbandmen (tenant farmers) and craftsmen. At the bottom of the heap were day-labourers or wage earners. The latter were people who had no land of their own to work and no specific occupation; they were full or part-time wage earners through casual employment. This was a large group since the use of casual labour was widespread. Presumably many mariners on the King's ships, such as the *Mary Rose*, came from this segment of the population. Indeed, it seems from contemporary assessments that there were only about 5,000 experienced mariners in England at any time in the early sixteenth century. No experience was necessary for ordinary mariners, and their pay was probably lower than that of the agricultural day-labourers[4]. These statements agree with what has been understood for many years about the nature of ships' crews[5] and they may well be true, at least for the early part of the reign. However, research on the human skeletal remains from the *Mary Rose* has provoked other ideas, as will be seen in Chapters 7 and 8.

The population of England had decreased from the Middle Ages onwards. The ravages of the plague returned, after 500 years, in the major outbreak of the Black Death in 1348. Almost the whole of Europe was involved in this pandemic which killed very large numbers of people. In England, at least one third of the population died during 1348 and 1349 and further outbreaks continued. The social and economic consequences were dramatic, with land lying uncultivated and a serious decline in trade and industry. The whole European economy became depressed, not only by the plague but also by the companion horrors of famine and war[6]. By the late fifteenth century, however, the population was stabilising and by the mid 1520's it was showing a slow but steady increase. This population was unevenly spread, with the greatest concentration of people in the East Midlands, East Anglia and the larger towns such as London; some rural areas, such as Devon, were also relatively densely populated. By the early sixteenth century there were about 45 people per square mile, averaged over the whole country. The total population is believed to have been about 2.3 million in 1525 and 2.8 million in 1541; this represented an increase of barely one per cent per annum, so growth was exceedingly slow. These population estimates may not be reliable, however, as Youings suggests[7]. Firstly, let us take the case of the 1525 estimate of 2.3 million.

In 1522, muster returns listed all able-bodied men, whatever their income, most clergy and some women[8]. The returns were intended to demonstrate both who was able and equipped to fight for the King and who was capable of being taxed. Since few of these returns survive, their use in estimating population is severely limited. The 1524–25 lay subsidies conducted an assessment of individual income of at least one pound per year in wages, land and goods. However, these subsidies omit income of less than one pound per year and exclude the clergy, most women and all children under the age of sixteen. Further, there are no surviving records from these assessments for the whole country and, even where they do survive, there are serious omissions. When the returns and the subsidies are compared for the few possible counties, there are serious discrepancies between the figures, thus suggesting that they are not useful sources for estimating early sixteenth century population.

In the case of the 1541 estimate, extrapolating evidence extracted from a non-random sample of just over four hundred parish registers derived this. These registers were started in 1538 and seem to have been intermittent in their recording. Registration was at the whim of the individual clerks and many people were excluded. Further, when they were copied in 1581, only the "most important" registers survived[9]. Thus, these records also present problems when used for the calculation of population size. However, given all the available evidence, it is probably reasonable to assume that the population of England in the latter part of Henry VIII's reign was about 2.5 or 3 million people.

The priorities of the vast majority of the sixteenth century population consisted of providing food and shelter for themselves and their families, from the land. Whilst there was a great diversity in land use, there were two main categories of agriculture, based on basic geography:

1. The older-settled 'fielden' or sheep-corn areas of mixed pasture and arable farming.

2. The relatively newly-settled 'forest' or wood-pasture of pastoral and dairy farming.

These categories were not based rigidly on the lowland areas of the south and east (1) and the higher, wetter areas of the north and west (2), but were much more mixed. There are, after all, areas of high ground in the south and east and of lowland in the north and west. However, the nature of the farming economy in any given region did determine the form of its settlements, so that in the fielden areas the population lived in nucleated villages with the farming areas outside the settlement, while in the forest areas people lived in hamlets or isolated farmsteads. Farming methods also differed in the two areas.

In fielden areas the arable land was still farmed communally and organised in the medieval system of unfenced strips (selions) of about one acre, usually in rectangular blocks (furlongs). The whole lot was organised into three great 'fields' of which two were cultivated and one was left fallow every year. Although these fields were farmed communally, the strips were owned individually and scattered over the whole arable area. Their boundaries were marked either by stones or wooden posts, or by narrow turf baulks[10]. In the forest areas farming was more specialised with no strips and few crops, the main concentration being on dairying and the grazing of large flocks of sheep on the open moorlands. Some echoes of this ancient farming system can be seen on the land today. For example, there is still evidence of strip farming on pasture which has not been deep-ploughed, particularly in the Midlands. Poor arable land was also enclosed very early in some areas, like Devon, and the small, erratically shaped fields with no strips which still survive are a record of this.

The population of early sixteenth century England was predominantly rural: only one person in twenty lived in a town. Large towns, such as London, could be regarded as cities, only recognising the King as their lord. These included places such as Bristol, York, Norwich and Exeter, all of which had populations of at least 5,000. London's population in 1500 was about 60,000. Many people worked at home and such homes/workshops were often on the outskirts of the town, in the suburbs. On the other hand, the country towns were really no more than big villages, which, unlike the cities, covered a large acreage. The larger villages had their own specialist craftsmen, such as wheelwrights, smiths, millers, carpenters and masons, as well as their backbone of agricultural labour. The towns supported even more craftsmen such as bakers, brewers, joiners, grocers and many others. The predominant secondary means of earning a living, however, was the making of woollen cloth and this activity gradually migrated from the towns into the villages and even on to isolated farms. Such secondary occupations were widespread and will have included, for men, seasonal work such as masonry, mining and quarrying as well as seafaring. It is probable that, for some at least of the mariners on the *Mary Rose*, their work on board ship was secondary to their work on the land. Whilst wages were paid to small sections of the working population, such as hired workmen, there was probably much payment in kind as well. For example, workers may have benefitted from the consumption of some of the foods they grew, as well as from the exploitation of common land, game and fishing[11]. Through most of England where there was any wealth or land to pass on, primogeniture was the rule by which the eldest son inherited the estate. Apart from the nobility and gentry, younger sons had to fend for themselves and, while many who were intellectually able went into the church (which provided a comfortable life at least until the dissolution), some gentlemen's sons were entrusted to ships' masters from the age of eleven[12]. There were at least two boys of about this age on the *Mary Rose* (see Chapter 5). Lawyers were always important professionals, and there was a large contingent of barristers at Westminster. In fact, the only two true professions in the early 1500's were those of Lawyers and Physicians. Their religion was of prime importance to all members of this society. The mystery plays spoke to everyone, telling them what they had to believe. Devotion to God and the Christian faith and membership of the Church were profound social duties, followed by all[13].

When Henry VIII suppressed the monasteries in the late 1530's, there were 800 religious houses within easy reach of all communities, containing a total of nearly 10,000 religious people of both sexes. The landed property that accompanied these communities was worth the astonishing figure of about £200,000 a year in the value of the time. Such property was spread over all counties and included all sizes and types. Although the first, smaller monasteries were suppressed in 1536, the Reformation really began in England in 1533–34 when Henry detached the English church from Rome[14]. He did this so that he could dissolve his first marriage to Catherine of Aragon, thus making their daughter Mary illegitimate, and marry Anne Boleyn, thus making her daughter Elizabeth legitimate. This detachment from Rome was purely expedient, since Henry was besotted with and determined to marry Anne and all other strategies had failed. However, he was always an orthodox and conservative man, and remained a Catholic in belief all his life[14].

Although prior to his attack on the monasteries there had been dissatisfaction with the church, its clergy and their wealth, the suppression of these houses paradoxically led to political unrest, particularly in the north. Apart from anything else, education and hospital care had been provided by the monastic church, and both of these suffered after the dissolution. General literacy remained poor, with only about 1 in 10 men even able to sign their names[15] and, although some hospitals survived, they only had residential provision for about 5,000 of the sick, due to the increased poverty of such houses.

Henry's other reason for suppressing the monasteries was in order to get his hands on their wealth and, from 1539 onwards, the Crown sold off the monasteries and their lands in order to finance the ongoing wars with France. These great sales led to profound changes in society, with yeomen now achieving the status of a new land-owning class.

Henry had first debased the coinage in 1526 to help pay for his wars, and he devalued it again in 1544, to support what would become his last war with France. Despite having inherited a stable, wealthy kingdom, by the end of his reign he had an unstable, fragmented country and large debts[16]. Apart from the King's persistent wars, there was also the problem of famine. Harvest failures, due to bad weather conditions, particularly excessive rain, tended to come in sequences and often after a run of good harvests. This was the case in 1527–28, when widespread harvest failure followed five good harvests in a row. Heavy winter rain had destroyed animals, pasture and cornfields and it then rained continuously from 12 April to 3 June, causing a failed harvest. The price of wheat rose higher than it had been since 1450 and its scarcity in the late 1520's was only exceeded by the later, awful harvests in 1556 and 1593–97[17]. Corn was used as breadcorn and as drinkcorn, along with other grains, and when it became extremely scarce people were driven either to hoard what little they had or, worse, to eat their seedcorn for the following year, when their other grains were gone. Thus, a disastrous harvest in one year could lead to another the next, due to a lack of planted crops. Nevertheless, the English fared better than many of their continental neighbours, such as France and Germany. Not only was the population much smaller but there were other sources of food particularly fish, meat and game. Since the basic subsistence diet seems to have been one of bread and ale, however, a serious dearth of wheat was clearly a problem. Severe harvest failure was often followed by serious outbreaks of plague so that 1527 and 1528 were both bad plague and disastrous harvest years. Whilst the men on the Mary Rose obviously survived those outbreaks of plague, evidence of the famines may be present on their skeletons. Obviously, famine causes severe nutritional deficiencies, which may leave evidence on the skeletons of the very young, such as the bowing of long bones which can accompany childhood rickets. Such evidence may survive into adulthood and this will be discussed in Chapter 7. Incidentally, had they not drowned on that summer evening in 1545, some of the crew might well have succumbed to a severe outbreak of plague, which attacked the Portsmouth area in August and September 1545.

THE ARMED FORCES

From 1511 onwards, all able-bodied men between the ages of sixteen and sixty were required to be equipped with suitable weapons, according to their status and their means, and to be able to use them skilfully. However, firearms were forbidden, except under licence, until 1544, although the practice of archery was encouraged. This may have had something to do with the King's interest in the sport. It was certainly the case that the English longbow man was, at his best, highly skilled in the use of the bow. Men were only required to muster with their weapons when either internal disorder or foreign invasion threatened; there was no standing army at this time. However, in times of need, armies had to come from somewhere to serve the King and these were provided, in a general sense, by retinues. Such private armies were illegal, except by royal licence, since they were a potential threat to the crown, especially in the hands of a powerful and ambitious lord. However, Henry VIII did not eradicate them and only proceeded against the private armies of two of his lords. He needed such ready-made armies for his wars[18]. Lists exist for the numbers of men and equipment mustered in retinues for the last war with France, which began in 1544. They include:

"Archers on foot": Duke of Suffolk = 100; Marquis of Dorset = 100; Earl of Essex = 150.

These were all to go to France with the King, along with other retinues, giving a total for the southern counties of 71,093 men and 18,552 harness (armour)[19]. There are, of course, no named individuals in these retinues. As in many other areas of life, only the great and the wealthy appear in written history. Yet, all the gentry in Tudor England represented only about two per cent of the population, and the merchant classes only about three per cent. Since these are the named individuals the vast majority of the population, about ninety-seven per cent, remains invisible and unrecorded, a point graphically illustrated elsewhere[20].

NOTES

1. Richardson defines such terms as 'demesne', 'seigniory' and 'seneschal'.
2. Landlords and tenants are discussed with clarity in Youings, chapter 2.
3. See Youings, p. 121.
4. Youings pp. 34 and 35.
5. For example, David Hannay talks about men being given a contract for only three months at a time and then returned to their villages.
6. See Slack's excellent text for a full discussion of plague and its consequences.
7. Youings, p. 132 *et seq.*
8. Campbell and Cornwall both discuss the musters and subsidies
9. Tiller, p. 146.
10. All the features of the medieval farming system are clearly described and identified in Richardson, especially sections A and B.
11. Livi-Bacci deals with the whole aspect of population, wages and nutrition.
12. Youings, pp. 35–7.
13. Brigden, p. 38.
14. Rodger p. 178. Interestingly, a number of rosaries were excavated from the *Mary Rose*, so it would appear that many other people shared Henry's beliefs.

15. Youings, p. 120.
16. Rodger p. 184.
17. See Dymond for a comprehensive description and discussion of the 1527 harvest failure in Essex and the south.
18. Youings, pp. 105–7.
19. L&P, vol. XIX, i; 1544: 273 R.O.
20. Hoskins 1964, *The Listener*.

FOUR

Crewing the King's Ships: Administration, Victualling and Pay

ADMINISTRATION

The largest personal Royal fleet since the Conquest was formed as a response to the political crises engendered by Henry VIII's ambitions and policies. The modern Royal Navy can trace a continuous history from this first war fleet, which was distinguished from its forerunners by its permanence and by its supportive administration[1]. Warships have always been large and expensive both to build and to maintain, and require a heavy investment in all their support systems, such as yards, stores, equipment and technical resources[1]. But, by the time of Henry's death, an administrative and logistical structure had been created which could support a permanent navy of warships. This structure was unique and, except possibly for that of Portugal, was the only such organisation outside the Mediterranean. The single most important achievement of sixteenth century England, in terms of sea power, was the creation of this naval administration, although it remained rudimentary for the greater part of the reign.

One office had been in existence since the fourteenth century, that of Keeper (Clerk) of the King's Ships. Robert Brigandyne had held this post since 1495 and he continued to do so until he retired in 1523. Although Brigandyne had no central role, he was involved in some naval administration, mainly at Portsmouth[2]. His successor was the Portsmouth dockmaster. Other, more important, naval responsibilities were given to whoever was available at the time. For example, the paymaster for the building of the *Great Harry* was William Bond, later Clerk of the Poultry in the Royal household, while the overseer was one of the Gentlemen of the Chapel Royal[2].

The origins of the future naval administration seem to have been in storekeeping and its centre was at Erith on the Thames, at least from 1514 until the 1540's. Henry's rapidly increasing fleet had to be supported and so during, and just after, the first French war of 1512–13 new storehouses were built at Erith and at Deptford, higher up the Thames estuary. Routine maintenance was carried out at Erith, probably because it was nearer to the sea than Deptford and more accessible for shipping, but it had disadvantages. For example, when the wind came from the northwest, it blew on to the anchorage and, in 1521, the door sills had to be raised by two feet to keep out the high tides[2]. In 1512, John Hopton, who was a court official, was appointed to act as Clerk Controller and to share administrative responsibility with Brigandyne. in 1514, he also became Keeper of the Storehouses at Erith and at Deptford. From this, he quickly became the most important figure in the incipient naval administration and was responsible for most of the naval expenditure by the time Brigandyne retired. In 1523, however, there was still no proper administrative structure nor permanent officials, except these two, and no budget.

Hopton died in 1524 and, at that time, Thomas Spert became Clerk Controller and William Gonson became Keeper of the Storehouses. Spert had been master of the *Mary Rose* and the *Great Harry* and was the first master and principal founder of Trinity House. He and Gonson were men of considerable substance, owning both ships and merchandise, as well as being experienced ships' masters. Gonson, one of the wealthiest citizens of London, was also an Exchequer official, an Admiralty Court Judge and a Vice-Admiral of Norfolk and Suffolk. Vice-Admirals of the Counties were appointed to look after the financial and legal interests of the Lord Admiral in the maritime counties; they were not usually sea commanders[3]. Gonson came to dominate the growing naval administration during the later 1520's and 1530's.

From 1525 to 1536, the Lord Admiral of England was the Duke of Richmond, the seven year old illegitimate son of the King, The young Duke's household was strongly influenced by the Lord Chancellor, Cardinal Wolsey, to whom Gonson reported[4]. Thus, naval administration was under the watchful control of the King's most powerful minister and, after his fall, that of his successor Thomas Cromwell. Both Wolsey and Cromwell informally controlled the navy through Gonson[5], who seems to have equipped and victualled fighting ships as well as paying the wages[6]. Spert, who was knighted in 1535 and died in 1541, appears to have had a more limited responsibility. In 1539, Gonson received the first small budget of £500 for the navy and, by the time he committed suicide in 1544, he was considered to be the paymaster of the fleet[7].

After the end of the first French war of 1512–13 Henry did not disperse his fleet, as had been the medieval custom. The big ships, at least, were maintained in readiness and Hopton's and Brigandyne's accounts record this maintenance and the expenditure it incurred. For example, in August 1518, the Mary Rose was caulked, at a cost of £100[8].

As well as the new storehouses, further docks were built at Portsmouth, Woolwich, Limehouse, Erith and Barking Creek. A second dock was built at Portsmouth in 1522–23, but the major innovation of this period was the building of the Deptford Pond. This was a large basin in which the King's great ships, including the *Mary Rose*, could lie afloat in reserve. By 1517, 22 of the King's ships were being maintained in the Thames estuary, each with its 'shipkeepers'[9]. By 1520, there seems to have been a standing navy, with a permanent fleet of about 30 ships, several dockyards and large storehouses. Mariners and craftsmen were hired by the day, week, or month according to the work available[10] but, as there was still no permanent administrative structure, real control remained in the hands of the King.

After Gonson's unexpected death during the last French war of 1544–46, his son Benjamin was appointed as acting treasurer. Davies suggests that, as Benjamin Gonson was appointed acting-successor to his father, it is unlikely that the latter's suicide had anything to do with corruption or dishonesty in his naval affairs. Rather, he considers it was probably influenced by the death by execution in 1541 of his other son, David, a knight of St. John[11]. By this time, the two positions occupied by Spert and Gonson had enlarged to three: Clerk of the Ships, Clerk Controller and Keeper of the Storehouse. Four more administrative positions were added by January 1545: Lieutenant (or Vice-Admiral) of the Admiralty, Treasurer, Surveyor and Rigger of Ships, and Master of Naval Ordnance[12]. The men occupying these posts constituted the 'Council of the Marine' or the 'Chief Officers of the Admiralty', under the chairmanship of the Vice Admiral. This was the future Navy Board[13]. The new structure represented the first true, permanent naval administration, with a well-defined hierarchy, properly paid officials and an administrative base at Deptford.

One official who has not yet been discussed is the Lord Admiral of England; his role mainly covered sea command. The post was usually held by active sea commanders such as Sir Edward Howard and his brother Lord Thomas, or by former naval officers like the Earl of Southampton. With only one exception, the Duke of Richmond, the Admiral was an experienced sea officer and, for most of the reign, he played little part in the administration of the navy. A marked change came in 1543 with the appointment of John Dudley, Viscount Lisle, as Henry's last Lord Admiral. Lisle had been a Vice-Admiral since 1537 and an active sea commander. He was a clever naval tactician but, unlike his predecessors, was also involved with naval administration ashore, working in close contact with William Gonson. Lisle's main duty, however, was command at sea and it was in this capacity, as Lord Admiral, that he was present on the *Great Harry* when the *Mary Rose* sank off Spithead on 19 July, 1545[14].

VICTUALLING AND PAY

An army marches and a navy sails on their respective stomachs. Keeping both an army and a navy fed has always presented problems, particularly before the advent of refrigeration and motorised transport. Armies in the sixteenth century, both by land and by sea, could be large. Henry VIII led 48,000 men into northern France in 1544, together with 20,000 horses; all had to be victualled[15]. In the same year, the expedition to Scotland gave estimates for an army by the sea of:

"15,000 men, mariners and soldiers, to be victualled for two months and to carry as much of the same in victuals with them as they can"[16].

These victuals presented problems both in quantity and in weight. For example, it was estimated that the provisions to be taken by a ship of 100 tons carrying 200 men for two 28-day months would take up so much space that the load would encroach on the ballast space, endangering the safety of the ship[16]. Therefore, a sixth of the victuals had to be left out in order for the ship to have the necessary 40 tons of ballast to "keep the sea". All the provisions were to be carried in 212 victualling support ships, totalling 7,500 tons and worked by 15,500 men[16]. The provisions, carts to carry them, men to work the victualling ships and the soldiers and mariners had all, of course, to be paid for. In addition, the victuals had to be transported from their region of origin to the port of loading, often on unreliable roads, and the victualling ships had then to wait for the right winds in order to sail to the fleet. All delays meant that food was liable to contamination and decay.

Life on board ship was neither comfortable nor easy, particularly for the ordinary soldier or sailor, who had:

"but to endure and suffer, as a hard cabin, cold and salt meat, broken sleeps, mouldy bread, dead beer, wet clothes, want of fire, all these within board"[17].

Conditions were a little better on the Royal ships, since they were less likely to be at sea for a long period of time and the larger ships were relatively more comfortable[18]. The men on these ships were also punctually paid and reasonably well fed[19]. Nevertheless, the life was still very tough and the severity of the mariners' and soldiers' lives was aggravated by the problems associated with supplying their food.

There was no full-time commissariat during the 1540's and a permanent organisation for the navy was not created until 1550. Before this, the victualling of a warship was the responsibility of the purser, who drew the money for this from the treasurer of the fleet. Food was stored and distributed by the steward, and prepared by the cook in the galley down in the hold[20]. The remains of such a galley were found and excavated on the *Mary Rose*, with parts of two brick-built ovens and their fire bases still present.

The victualling arrangements for Henry's large fleets were improvised and disorganised. The main responsibility for victualling lay with the government, and supplies were raised by purveyance – the royal right to buy at fixed prices[21]. This was unpopular for three reasons:

1. It caused local price rises by driving up demand.
2. It was open to abuse by purveyors in terms of both poor quality and short measure.
3. The crown was only a sporadic payer, providers often waiting a long time for payment[22].

The crown also tried to keep costs down by depressing the price of victuals. Provisions were carried on board a warship but, due to pressure of space and problems of preservation, English warships could only stow victuals for three or four months[23].

The rate of victualling a mariner in 1545 was 18d (eighteen pence in Tudor money) a week, and two months provisions were estimated to occupy 83 tons of space in a 100 ton ship with 200 mariners and soldiers[24]. Oppenheim discusses the food allowances for each man per day, stating that a pound of biscuit and a gallon of beer were allowed and '200 pieces of flesh' to every 100 men on four days of the week[24]. However, in 1565 a standard ration, based on 4½d a day when in harbour and 5d a day at sea, was provided for each man. It consisted of:

A gallon of beer and a pound of bread per day (fresh bread when in port, biscuit when at sea). On four flesh days either two pounds of fresh beef, half-a-pound of salt beef or half-a-pound of bacon; on three fish days (Wednesday, Friday and Saturday), either a quarter of a stockfish (dried cod) or four herrings. Four ounces of butter and half-a-pound of cheese were also provided[21]. Wherever possible, the men supplemented this diet with fresh foods, such as fruit and vegetables. The excavation of the *Mary Rose* yielded barrels of butchered meat bones, including beef and pork and trimmed fish bones[25]. Peppercorns were also found in some of the chests and in a wooden peppermill in the surgeon's cabin[26].

The bulk of all this food was capable of preservation for a short while, by drysalting, drying and packing in salt pickle. The lack of proper preservation always caused problems, however, leading to shortages, sickness, enfeeblement and scurvy[27]. Even the beer, which was brewed without hops, went sour very quickly, causing enteritic problems, especially in hot weather[27]. Thus, the dysentery in August 1545 in the ships at Portsmouth was caused, according to Suffolk and Lisle, by corrupted food[28]. Equally, of the £26,000 worth of food (in Tudor money) which the Boulogne garrison received in 1545–46, over £11,000 worth had to be destroyed because it was rotten[28]. So, the victualling of the fleet was a major problem in the sixteenth century. It was also an expensive business.

A great deal of money was required to build, arm, and maintain the Royal ships, and to feed and pay their crews. Out of £699,000 which Henry VIII spent in 1513, the naval expenses from 4th March to 31st October were £23,000[29]. Since these figures are in sixteenth century values, there were clearly very large sums involved. All revenues were, of course, directly in the hands of the King and the monies were only spent on his orders. Several thousand pounds a year continued to be spent on the navy throughout the reign and, during the 1540's, this expenditure became very large. For example, the naval expenses from September 1542 to Henry's death in 1547 were £262,462. Of this, the largest amount, £127,846, was paid out in wages, followed by £65,610 in victualling[30]. These monies, which Henry spent so freely, came from the suppression of the monasteries but, as the revenues were only £250,000 and Henry was spending £650,000 a year, he was running up large foreign debts[31], which he never cleared.

From the latter half of the fifteenth century, a mariner's wage was 5s (five shillings) a month in Tudor money, and it stayed at this rate for nearly the whole of Henry VIII's reign[32]. In addition to this pay, there were a number of supplements. Victuals were provided, and also conduct money from a man's home village to the port and back. Sometimes, jackets or coats were also made available, usually in the Tudor colours of green and white[33]. For example, when the *Peter Pomegranate* and the *Mary Rose* were brought round from Portsmouth to the Thames in 1510 to be fitted-out, 34 green and white coats were provided for 24 soldiers and 10 officers at a cost of 6s 10d each[34]. Similarly, when Sir Edward Howard indented to raise, pay, feed and clothe the entire fleet in 1512, he had to provide the mariners with coats at 1s 8d each, charging for 1,616 of them, as well as for 1,812 coats for the soldiers[35]. Presumably, these coats were for the officers, since the numbers of mariners and soldiers in the whole fleet far exceeded those supplied with coats. There are references in 1513 to 1,244 "mariners', gunners' and servitors'" jackets, and to 638 coats of white and green cloth, 13 of white and green camlet (a light cloth made of various materials), four coats of satin and one of damask[35]. Although the references to mariners' clothing become fewer during the century, the provision of jackets seems to have continued until the end of the reign, since there is a reference in 1545 to the possibility of providing 1,800 mariners with coats at 2s each[35].

Another income supplement, which largely benefitted the officers, was provided by the distribution of 'deadshares'. Under this system, which was introduced by Henry VIII and continued until 1695, fictitious names were entered into the ship's muster book, allowing the captain to draw 'ghost' sea pay of 5s per name or share, which was then distributed among the officers[36]. The number of shares, of course, depended on the size of the ship. The naval expenses for 1513 mention 27½ deadshares allowed to the master and mariners of the *Mary Rose* at 5s a deadshare[37]. Oppenheim states that, for a month of 28 days in the *Peter Pomegranate*, the master obtained £1 10s, the master's mate and the quartermasters 10s, the boatswain 12s 6d, the master gunner, carpenter, steward and cook 10s, and the gunners 6s 8d, on top of their basic 5s a month[38]. By 1582, the master of a ship of the size of the *Mary Rose* was receiving a total of £2 per 28-day month[39] and, before the end of Henry's reign, a certain number of deadshares seem to have been divided between the mariners as well.

In response to the need to enlist 5,000 men for the war, the King raised the basic mariner's wage in 1545 from 5s a month to 6s 8d[40]. This rate remained the same for most of the rest of the century, at least on the Royal ships, although the wages in the merchant service varied between 5s and 8s a month, and are estimated to have risen to 10s by the 1560's[41]. There is also some evidence that sick men were still paid and that discharged disabled mariners sometimes received gratuities[42]. For example, under the naval expenses for 1513 is the item:

"Andrew Fysche, one of the gunners of the Mare Roose to heal him of his hurts 13s 4d"[43].

NOTES

1. Rodger p. 221.
2. *Op. cit.*, p. 222.
3. *Op. cit.*, p. 298.
4. *Op. cit.*, p. 223.
5. *Ibid.*
6. Opp. p. 84.
7. Rodger, *op. cit.*
8. Loades, p. 69.
9. *Op. cit.*, p. 71. Loades says (footnote 2, p. 70) that: "At this date the masters of all but the smallest ships were retained as shipkeepers, usually with 2–4 mariners".
10. *Op. cit.*, p. 73.
11. Davies: Administration of the Royal Navy, p. 275, footnote.
12. Loades, p. 81.
13. Rodger, p. 225; Davies *op. cit.*, p. 275.
14. A list of Admirals and Officials is given in Rodger, Appendix V.
15. Davies: Provisions for Armies, p. 234.
16. L&P 19, i): 140. R.O. St. P., v., 338, 5. 1544
17. Rodger, p. 319.

18. Loades, pp. 34 and 54.
19. Opp. p. 74.
20. Loades, p. 34-5.
21. Rodger, p. 235.
22. Davies, *op. cit.*, pp. 236–8.
23. Rodger, p. 236.
24. Opp., p. 82.
25. Jenny Coy, personal communication, 2000.
26. MRT 3, p. 30.
27. Kemp, p. 5.
28. Rodger, p. 234.
29. Opp. p. 93.
30. *Op. cit.*, p. 94.
31. Rodger, pp. 236–7.
32. Opp. p. 75.
33. Loades, p. 99.
34. L&P 1, i), 3608: Daunce's accounts.
35. Opp. p. 76.
36. Loades, *op. cit.*
37. L&P 1, i), 2478.
38. Opp. p. 75.
39. Rodger, p. 500.
40. Loades, p. 98.
41. Hair and Alsop, p. 123.
42. Opp. p. 76.
43 L&P 1, i), 2305 iii.

FIVE

Crewing the King's Ships: Officers and Men

SHIPBOARD OFFICERS

The definition of the term 'officer' in the sixteenth century was different from that employed today; it also varied widely according to the size of the ship and her function[1]. As well as the captain (in overall charge and, on a warship, in control of the soldiers) and the master (in charge of the mariners and the handling of the ship), a warship's 'officers' generally consisted of ranks that we might consider to be those of 'petty officers' in the modern navy. The main ranks were those of boatswain, carpenter, master gunner, purser and surgeon. Generally, the master, boatswain, carpenter and gunner each had a mate, and bigger ships (such as the *Great Harry* and the *Mary Rose*) also had other junior officers, such as quartermasters. In overall command at sea was the Lord Admiral or his deputy the Lieutenant of the Admiralty (Vice-Admiral). Admirals and Vice-Admirals were (and are now) known as flag officers and their ships as flagships. The flagship would fly the Royal Standard[2]. As we have seen, (Chapters 1 and 4), Lord Lisle was Lord Admiral in 1545 and his flagship was the *Great Harry*. Sir George Carew, the Vice-Admiral, was also present on his flagship, the *Mary Rose*, on July 19th. Carew seems to have been appointed Vice-Admiral "of that journey"[3]. In other words, the appointment may have been temporary for that particular campaign. Thus, the *Mary Rose* would have been Carew's flagship and the Anthony Roll clearly shows her flying the Royal Standard (see figure 4). Just before she sailed, the King appears to have given Carew his own gold chain and whistle as a badge of office[3]. Such a whistle is known as a 'Boatswain's Call' or 'Pipe' and was used traditionally both as a badge of office and, in a larger size, to pipe orders around the ship by the use of various tones. Nowadays, the instrument is used ceremonially to pipe important people aboard a Royal Navy ship.

Four Boatswain's Calls were recovered from the *Mary Rose* in two sizes: either less than two inches or between four and six inches in length. The smaller form seems to have been the badge of rank and the larger form the working instrument[4]. Two of these Calls recovered from the ship came from a chest on the main deck at the stern. One was the largest of the four (168mm, 6.6 inches long), the other was in fragments. Only one of the other Calls (138mm, nearly 5.5 inches, long) was associated with skeletal material and it is likely to have been one of the working instruments. It was found on the main deck, amidships, and will be discussed later together with the associated skeleton[5]. None of the Calls was gold, suggesting that the one the King gave Carew was not recovered. However, the smallest, only 60mm (2.4 inches) long, would seem to have been a badge of office. This was recovered from the main deck at the stern and, as Carew was last recorded as seen above decks (see Chapter 2), was probably not his. Since Calls were also carried by masters, captains, boatswains and quartermasters, it probably belonged to another officer.

The captain of the *Mary Rose* was young Roger Grenville, son of Sir Richard Grenville 'the Elder' and father of the famous Sir Richard of the Revenge, who was only an infant in July 1545. Like Sir George Carew, Roger Grenville died on the *Mary Rose*[6]. He also, like Carew, came from an established and distinguished West Country family of rank and would have been a gentleman. The captain of a large Royal warship was always a knight or a gentleman from the court and was appointed by the King[7]. As the reign progressed, however, such men became less freely available to the navy and those of a lesser social rank were given the command of some of the King's ships. Although not courtiers, these men were often established and experienced seamen and ship owners[8] and many came from the West Country. They included such men as Thomas Spert, John Hopton and William Gonson. The captain was in general control of the ship and her voyage, as well as her contingent of soldiers, some of whom may have come aboard as his own retinue. These 'soldiers of the sea' were the fore-runners of the modern marines and were under the direct command of the captain. The sailing of the ship, however, and the organisation of the mariners was under the control of the master who, like the officers mentioned above, would be from a lower social class than the captain[9]. Thus, the shipboard hierarchy reflected the hierarchy on land. Therefore, on the *Mary Rose*, the Vice-Admiral would have been in overall command at the top, followed by the captain, the master and other officers, while at the bottom were the soldiers and mariners.

The masters of English ships were, until the 1550's, basically coastal pilots and the English, unlike the Scots, Portuguese and Spanish remained essentially tied to coastal waters, rather than venturing farther afield[10]. This was a function of the poor quality of navigation, coupled with an inability to calculate longitude. The master was normally responsible for his own navigation, at least in the merchant service[11]. Three cabins were found on the main deck during the excavation of the hull of the ship and:

"the roles of those who used them have been suggested by the artefacts found inside each cabin"[12].

So, it is assumed that the cabins belonged to the pilot, the carpenter and the barber surgeon (figure 7). Simple navigational equipment, probably belonging to the pilot, was recovered from the area of his cabin on the main deck in the bow of the *Mary Rose*. A gimballed compass, along with personal items and clothing, came from a fine dovetailed elm chest. In addition to the compass, a pine plotting board and two pairs of dividers were found in this cabin. Whether the pilot on the *Mary Rose* was also the master is uncertain. There are various references to the fact that, since very few ships carried a pilot, the master in most ships was responsible for the navigation[13]. This may, however, have applied largely to merchant ships and not to warships. Another, damaged, chest recovered from the aftercastle area of the upper deck, contained, among other things, a further gimballed compass, small lead weights and two pairs of copper alloy dividers[14]. It has been suggested that there may have been a second pilot on board or, alternatively, that the same pilot may have owned both chests[14]. Another possibility is that the aftercastle chest may have belonged to the master who owned some navigational equipment, particularly as his quarters are likely to have been in this area of the ship.

The master gunner, the boatswain and the carpenter were among the

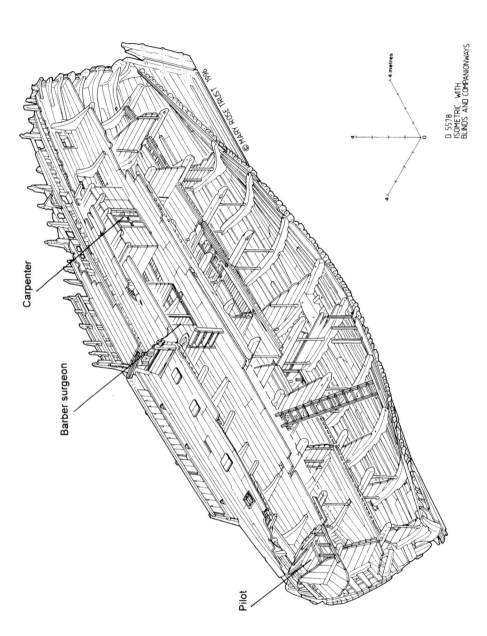

Figure 7. An isometric projection of the *Mary Rose*, showing the main features of the surviving hull and the location of the cabins. Copyright © the Mary Rose Trust.

most important officers on a warship. A master gunner was highly skilled in his trade and, therefore, much in demand, unlike the gunners on a merchantship who were usually ordinary mariners with some skill in handling the guns. By contrast, a warship's master gunner had to know everything about his guns and their performance. In addition, he had complete responsibility for guns, ammunition, magazines and all associated equipment. When necessary, for example in a rough sea, it was his responsibility to ensure that the lower deck guns were hauled in and the gun ports closed and sealed[15]. A boatswain, on the other hand, was usually a former mariner who had risen to his rank by experience. He was responsible for transmitting the master's orders to the crew, by means of his Call, clearing the decks for action, stowing cargo and ballast and for the general good running of the ship. He usually had his own mate, stood watches at sea and often went on to become a master himself. In the sixteenth century merchant service, the average age of a boatswain was 27[16]. Ships' carpenters were highly-skilled men who had almost certainly served an apprenticeship, either at sea or on land, in a shipyard. Scammell suggests that the carpenter was one of the most important men on a ship, since he supervised maintenance of the ship's structure and was instrumental in carrying out emergency repairs[11]. Thus, the fate of the ship and her crew could depend upon his skill.

Rodger[15] states that the master gunner, the boatswain and the carpenter were "perhaps the least educated" of a warship's officers. However, some of the evidence from the excavation of the *Mary Rose* seems to question this statement. Inside the carpenter's cabin was a dovetailed walnut chest containing:

> "valuable and highly regarded items .... suggesting a literate owner of some status and wealth"[14]

These items included pewter plates, a leather book cover, silver coins and rings and a sundial in a leather case, as well as some carpentry equipment. Of two other chests in this cabin, one contained the remains of tools and the other the remains of clothing. An oak chest with a carved front found outside the carpenter's cabin also contained valuable items, including silver coins and rings, one of the Calls referred to above, an engraved copper-capped knife handle, a pair of shoes and a leather book cover. Again, it is suggested that the owner was a comparatively wealthy and literate man and the presence of a carved linstock and copper alloy priming wire "suggest that he might be a master gunner"[14]. So, it is possible that both the master gunner and the carpenter on the *Mary Rose* were literate and wealthy men.

English ships during the sixteenth century seem to have had a high proportion of officers to men. As well as the basic ranks named above, other occupations such as those of cook, smith, tailor, shoemaker, trumpeter and musician were represented on many ships; presumably, these were the equivalent of modern petty officers[17]. Clearly musicians were present on the *Mary Rose*, since a tabor drum and pipes were found in the crew's quarters astern of the main mast and a shawm (a form of oboe) was found close to the barber surgeon's cabin on the main deck[18]. Many tools were also found amongst the more than 19,000 artefacts recovered from the ship, representing a variety of crafts and occupations.

Another important officer on board a warship, for morale as well as his possible medical skills, was the ship's surgeon. In Tudor society, there were four distinct categories of medical practitioner [19]:

1. Physicians, who were the most prestigious and had degrees from Oxford or Cambridge.

2. Members of the Fellowship of Surgeons, who were usually university trained and often held dual qualifications, allowing them to practise both surgery and medicine. Watt states very definitely that these men were highly trained and qualified. On the other hand, Gosse remarks that "it is probable that the standard of skill required by a ship (*sic*) surgeon was much lower than that needed for practice among the civil population at home".[20]

3. Barber surgeons of the Barbers' Company, who served either a seven or a nine year apprenticeship to a master surgeon followed by a qualifying examination, in order to practise. (The barbers in the Company only practised barbering, although sometimes a naval barber-surgeon was required to practise both skills.)

4. Apothecaries, who sold medicines and ointments from their shops, and offered free advice to ordinary citizens.

Figure 8. Holbein's painting of the presentation of the Charter to the newly amalgamated Company of Barber Surgeons in 1540.
Courtesy of the Worshipful Company of Barbers.

Henry had surrounded himself with able and intellectually impressive medical men, many of whom appear in the famous painting by Holbein of Henry granting the Charter to the newly affiliated Company of Barbers and Surgeons in 1540 (figure 8). In this painting, the King's royal physicians, Dr. John Chambre and Dr. William Butts are on his right hand, with the royal apothecary, Thomas Alsop, behind. Thomas Vicary, serjeant-surgeon, Sir John Ayliff, surgeon to the King and Nicholas Simpson, king's barber, are directly on Henry's left. Other barbers and surgeons, some named, also appear on the King's left (figure 8). An act of 1511 required all physicians and surgeons to be licensed by the church before they could practise. Although this was amended in 1543, to broaden the requirements so that more men could practise, the surgeons who served in the 1545 fleet were trained under the original, stricter, act[19].

According to Watt, there seems to have been some established organisation for providing surgeons and even physicians on warships by the 1540's. For example, the first mention of surgeons at sea appears in the Exchequer Accounts for 1513, which list 32 naval surgeons serving under four masters[21]. A chief surgeon called Robert Sympson, assisted by Henry Yonge, is listed as serving in the *Mary Rose.* The selection of naval surgeons was much more rigorous than for the army and was, until the nineteenth century, the special responsibility of the Barber Surgeons Company and its successor, the Royal College of Surgeons. Although there is no extant list of surgeons for the 1545 fleet, the organisation of medical facilities at the time was probably similar to that of the 1513 fleet, with the appointment of experienced master surgeons, for the campaign only, in the largest ships. It seems likely that the officer on the *Mary Rose* would have been a well-qualified master surgeon and a senior member of the Company; he would have been assisted by one or more barber surgeons[22].

Watt argues[22] that Tudor surgeons followed sound surgical principles with an emphasis on cleanliness. Apparently head injuries, closed and compound fractures, dislocations, wounds and serious burns were "often treated admirably" and amputations could be performed "with minimal blood loss". Haemorrhage was controlled by the use of pressure, styptics or ligature. Their methods were probably based on those taught and practised in Bologna and included the removal of missiles and fragments from wounds, the stitching of wounds and the use of anaesthesia or analgesia with soporific sponges impregnated with opium, hyocyamine (from henbane), hemlock, mandragora, lettuce, mulberry and ivy juice[19]. One of the three identified cabins on the Mary Rose belonged to the surgeon. It was on the main deck near many of the battle stations (see figure 7). Inside this cabin was a four-legged oak plank with a tapering top, identified as a 'plastering bench' and, outside, was a folding oak stand which, with the addition of a board, could have functioned as a table[23]. Among the other things in this cabin was a walnut chest with elm handles containing about sixty items[12]. These included turned poplar canisters containing ointment, and pine spatulas for spreading it, rolls of fine fabric impregnated with ointment (probably prepared on the 'plastering bench'), stoneware medicine bottles with corks, a probable feeding bottle and the remains of a possible trepan, a brass syringe, wooden bowls, and the handles for scalpels and knives, the steel blades of which had been destroyed by corrosion (figure 9). Chemical and microscopic analysis of some of these items revealed the presence of a wide variety of materials, which were used medicinally. They include such things as fern oil, pine resin, frankincense, beeswax, mercury and plant oils. [A full description of these can be found in Castle, J. (2005) 'Septicaemia, Scurvy and the Spanish pox: provisions for sickness and injury at sea'; chapter 4 in J. Gardiner (ed) 'Before the Mast: life and death aboard the *Mary Rose*'. Portsmouth: Mary Rose Trust (The

Figure 9. Some of the contents of the surgeon's chest/cabin, excavated from the ship.
Copyright © the Mary Rose Trust.

Archaeology of the *Mary Rose*, Volume 4)]. There were other items in the cabin, which would have been used by the surgeon. These included a wooden mallet, probably used with chisels and bone gauges and another, pewter, syringe. It has been suggested that the two syringes were used for the treatment of gonorrhea[24]. However, Watt argues that such syringes would have been used for irrigating wounds and drainage tracks and that venereal disease was not a serious problem in the fleet until the later, longer voyages[22]. The prevalence of venereal disease is, of course, unknown in the fleet at this time and so it is difficult to understand the logic of his argument. Two delicate, fluted glass bottles which were probably originally encased in silver were also found, and two finely engraved bone scoops "for removing wax from the ears" [Watt, p. 12. Earwax was collected and kept as a cheaper alternative to beeswax for coating string and thread in order to waterproof it]. Watt suggests that these artefacts, together with a silk velvet coif similar to those worn by the senior surgeons in the Holbein painting (figure 8), indicate that the surgeon was "a man of some standing". The surgeon would obviously have been a literate man; the fine artefacts described above would suggest that he was also probably of high status within his profession.

There were no human skeletal remains in the surgeon's cabin and his chest was found prepared, but sealed and unused. This is something of an enigma, as the ship was going into battle when she sank. However, Watt suggests (see Chapter 2) that there may have been sick men in the hold and that the surgeon and his mate could have been tending to them there. It is certainly the case that, by early August 1545, there was an epidemic of dysentery in the fleet which was serious enough for Lisle and Suffolk to write to the King about it[25]. Watt suggests that the *Mary Rose* may have been one of the first ships to be struck by this epidemic and that her medical team was attending to the most serious cases in the hold.

SHIPBOARD MEN

According to the Anthony Roll, the total crew of the *Mary Rose* consisted of 200 mariners, 185 soldiers and 30 gunners[26]; there is no indication as to how many, or which, of these men were the officers. Other estimates of the crew size vary widely. Oppenheim speaks of :

  "200 soldiers, 180 sailors and 20 gunners"[27],

  Loades says that she sank with the loss of about:

  "500 soldiers and seamen"[28],

while McKee calculated a total of 530, by adding on 15 Admiral's staff and an extra company of infantry to the basic 415 on the Anthony Roll[29]. Finally, there is the apocryphal tale that an extra 300 men were on board on the day she sank (see Chapters 1 and 2). So, estimates of the ship's company vary from a total of 415 men to a rather unlikely 715. The problem is compounded by the fact that there are no naval records from this date, so it is not possible to know the true figure. What is certain, however, is that ships at this time were grossly over-manned, a natural consequence of the high prevalence of disease, accident and death, together with the labour-intensive operation of a ship[33]. In 1534, some ships were so overmanned that the men to tonnage ratios could be as high as 1:3 or even 1:2[30]. An action station list from the *Great Harry*, of unknown date, gives one man to every two tons of burthen[31]. Rodger argues, however, that some of these men must have been soldiers, since this ratio is far too high[32]. In the early years of Henry's reign, ships' companies were still recruited as indentured retinues so that, in 1512–13, the whole fleet was technically the personal retinue of Sir Edward Howard who indented to raise, pay, feed and clothe it himself[33]. Soldiers outnumbered mariners by at least 2:1 in such companies. By the 1540's, the proportions of men had changed, with fewer soldiers and more mariners. For example, a document of 1513 states that the *Mary Rose* had 200 soldiers, 180 sailors and 20 gunners[27] whereas in 1545, while the total was similar, the proportions had changed to 185 soldiers, 200 mariners and 30 gunners, a ratio of one man to every three tons burthen[34]. This ratio demonstrates the sixteenth century's extravagance in manning, when it is compared to the 1938 figure of 1 man to every 100 tons burthen for the whole fleet[30]. The change between 1513 and 1545 was probably a reflection of the perceived need for more sailors as fighting tactics at sea changed, becoming based on speed and manoeuvre rather than on grappling and hand-to-hand fighting. By this time, however, the national population of mariners was decreasing. Even when the King raised the mariner's basic wage from 5s to 6s 8d a month in 1545, the rewards from privateering and its profit sharing were still greater[34].

Henry was able to recruit mariners with no difficulty in the early part of his reign. In May 1514 the main battle fleet was manned by 3,982 seamen and 447 gunners as well as soldiers[34]. By 1544, however, it was much more difficult, with the occurrence of shortages and even desertions[34]. The problem was caused partly by an increase in the numbers of ships during the reign and partly by competition from privateering. Disease also presented a considerable problem. For example, in 1545 during the first two weeks of September, Lisle lost more than a quarter of his 12,000 men to plague[35]. (Disease continued to be a significant problem: in 1588, a ship was fumigated by burning wet broom[36]. Broom was found during the excavation of the *Mary Rose*. It, too, may have been used as a fumigant, although the more likely explanation is that it was tied in bundles and used to scrub down the decks[37]).

At the time, the shortage of mariners was attributed to the decay of the port towns and of the fishing fleet. Although this may have been a factor, some ports, such as Newcastle, were actually flourishing[38]. The result of the acute shortage of seamen was that men were recruited for the crown by the ancient practice of impressment, by which they were ordered to travel, unescorted, to the nearest port to serve on the King's ships. There is evidence that conduct money was paid to impress men for travel both to and from the port[39]. Impressment was used even at the beginning of the reign. In April, and again in October of 1512, men were paid conduct money of 6d per day to travel from their homes:

"to the place of shipment, accounting 12 miles for a day's journey"[40].

Benjamin Gonson's accounts in 1544 list, among others, conduct money for mariners as well as payments for masters and gunners, all from John Ryther, the King's Cofferer[41]. Impressment was only used in wartime and there is, of course, a modern equivalent in compulsory national service. Not all men were imprest – some volunteered, while others came from the fishing boats[42]. Some crews came from enemy ships, such as those of the French and the Scots, which were taken as prizes in action and their crews then imprest for service with the English fleet[43]. In addition to the impressment of men, merchant ships were taken for Royal service during wartime[41], and Henry also hired some foreign ships[44].

Although there is a long tradition of seafaring in the West Country, it cannot necessarily be assumed that the majority of the crew members on the King's ships were from Devon and Cornwall. Both Carew and Grenville came from the region, and may have brought some of their own men with them, but men were also brought from many other places to serve the King. Devon had over ten per cent of the whole country's active ships' masters and 16 per cent of the national total of ordinary mariners in the later part of the century. Nevertheless, in 1545, there were not enough mariners in the area to crew new ships[45]. Numbers of mariners for the whole country are difficult to gauge. Some fragmentary returns show 550 seamen in the East Anglian ports in 1536, while Dorset had 255 mariners in 1543[46]. However, records are sparse for this period so that the recorded number of seamen does not truly reflect the total manpower serving in both merchantmen and warships.

Men recruited from maritime counties and rural communities often went to sea as a secondary occupation, their other work being associated with agriculture. Men from different areas will have had various secondary occupations, being described as 'yeoman or mariner', 'grocer or mariner', for example[47]. Many mariners did not come from a maritime family or begin their careers at sea; they came from a variety of backgrounds and from many different areas. For example, of 35 London seamen, seven were from the West Country, nine from the south-east, nine from Yorkshire and Lincolnshire, three from the Midlands, three from the north-east, two from Calais, and one each from Scotland and Ireland[48]. There was a lot of mobility among seamen with constant movement from port to port. Crews were also cosmopolitan and could include Flemings, Italians, Dutchmen and Greeks[48]. While much of this is recorded for merchant shipping, clearly it was also true for Royal ships. In January 1545, 200 Spaniards were prest into service for Henry in Falmouth[49] and, in February of the same year, Italian soldiers were to be enlisted for Henry's war. Similarly, 600 starving Flemings were prest into service from their own ships, driven into Falmouth by foul weather and no victuals[50]. In July, 1545, Van der Delft wrote to Charles V (the Emperor) that he was told:

"by a Fleming among the survivors"

how the *Mary Rose* had been sunk[51]. So, the Royal warships, like the merchant ships, were probably crewed by men from a very wide area and a large variety of backgrounds.

Sixteenth century mariners were predominately young. The tough conditions and dangers of shipboard life meant that it only attracted young and ambitious men who had not much to lose. These men were largely unmarried and with no permanent homes, but with lodgings in port[52]. The evidence is sparse, but the survival of a few statistics shows that, in the middle of the century, the majority of seamen were under 40, and probably under 30.

These figures are similar to those of today, where ordinary seamen are still predominately young. There is one important difference, however.

Table 1: Ages of seamen (taken from Scammell: Manning, p 138)

	Under 20	20–30	31–40	41–50	51+
c. 1535–50	1	30	6	1	2

It is likely that a ship would have a boy as young as 11 on board in the sixteenth century[46]. Some boys were apprenticed to a master for seven years or more, to be trained as a mariner or in the art of navigation. Many were the sons of craftsmen, merchants, yeomen or even gentlemen[53]. The Bristol Apprentice Register of 1532–1658 records some of these boys. In 1537–38, four of the bound apprentices of William Spratt, woolmerchant, were taken to be trained as mariners; in 1543, Thomas Phelps, son of a shipmaster, and Robert Gay, son of a merchant, were both apprenticed to the sea, Phelps to a shipmaster and Gay to a 'maryner'[54]. The master or his mate in such cases would do the training. Boys from poorer backgrounds would not have the security of an apprenticeship but would have to 'learn the ropes' as best they could. Rodger says that, apart from this, there is little evidence of what such boys did, although they may have been stationed in the fighting tops, as lookouts[55]. Apprenticed boys became skilled officers and were groomed for command, if they survived the sea. Those who were friends or relatives of the rich and powerful were, in general, the ones who were given commands when rather young[56]. Thus, Roger Grenville, the captain of the Mary Rose when she sank, was a young commander and his father, 'old' Sir Richard, a prominent and wealthy man.

Some ages of masters have been recorded (Table 2) and these show that the largest numbers were in the age range 31 to 40.

The few statistics that survive for the other officers suggest average ages of 30 for a master's or principal mate, 27 for a boatswain and 30 for a quartermaster,[57] again demonstrating the relative youthfulness of a ship's company. The relationship of all the recorded ages to those for the crew of the Mary Rose will be discussed later.

Seamen were generally reviled for their brawling and drunkeness ashore and there are numerous examples of this behaviour, such as the following:

Table 2. Ages of 36 masters (taken from Scammell: Manning, p 147)

20–30	31–40	41–50	51–60	60+
8	14	7	5	2

"In 1539, some seamen from the warship *Mary Rose* jubilantly returning from a night's drinking and unable (or so they said) to get aboard, helped themselves to a wherry, rammed a Portuguese merchantman, and having received a rough reception from its crew boarded it, 'purposing', as they later explained 'to give them a blow or two'"[58].

On 19th July, 1545, Sir George Carew had, apparently,

". . . the kind of knaves I cannot rule"

aboard the *Mary Rose* when she sank. As we have seen, the sinking has often been attributed to drunkeness or insubordination of one kind or another. Nonetheless, the sea also attracted men of ambition, talent and character and many, like Drake, rose from very humble beginnings (he was born in poverty near Tavistock in Devon) to rank and wealth. There was also, perhaps surprisingly, a high standard of literacy among some seamen and the majority could understand and use written documents[59]. This is an interesting point. Another study suggests that, at the time of Queen Elizabeth's accession in 1558, illiteracy in the adult male population was about 80 per cent and that, for the years 1788–1815, between 40 per cent and 50 per cent of British merchant seamen were illiterate[60]. Of course, the true levels of literacy on the *Mary Rose* are unknown but there are certainly some artefacts, such as bowls and a tig (tankard), which have distinctive marks on them, probably made by the owner. On the other hand, some artefacts would seem to suggest a higher standard of literacy among the crew. For example, there is a knife handle and a trencher, both of which are incised with a letter 'W' on them; similarly, a wooden eating spoon has a reversed letter 'N' on the underside of the bowl[61].

Many seamen were highly skilled and, although not wealthy, often had a reasonable wardrobe in their sea chests; many of the chests recovered from the *Mary Rose* contain vestiges of clothing (see Richards). They wore short jerkins ('petti-coats'), shirts, stockings and loose breeches ('slops'). Gowns, cassocks and capes could be worn in bad weather. There are some references to hats and caps, boots and shoes[59] and examples of both the latter were recovered from the wreck of the *Mary Rose*. Some livery coats in the Tudor colours of green and white were worn on the *Mary Rose* when she was first commissioned, but this seems to have been abandoned later[59, 62].

WHO WERE THE MEN OF THE *MARY ROSE?*

When the *Mary Rose* was excavated on the seabed before being raised, a considerable amount of human skeletal material was found within the wreck. This material is unique, since it represents the only existing sample of a group of Tudor individuals available for study. Usually, such remains from a period as late as the sixteenth century are still in cemeteries and it is therefore not possible for archaeologists to excavate them or for them to be available for study. However, because of the circumstances of their burial as part of a shipwreck, the human skeletal remains from the *Mary Rose* became available for specialist examination and research. Such research has provided valuable information about the crew of one of Henry VIII's Great Ships, and allowed interesting speculation regarding some of the occupations which may have been followed by these crew members. The names of two individuals who were on the ship when she sank are already known: the Vice Admiral, Sir George Carew and the captain, Roger Grenville and, given the unique nature of the surviving burials, there are strong arguments for trying to find evidence for the identities of other crew members.

Some documentary evidence, naming a number of the *Mary Rose*'s officers, is available for the years 1511–1514. For example, John Clerke was master of the ship from July to September of 1511[63] while, from October 1511 to 1513, there are various references to Thomas Spert as her master[64]. There is also a record of Spert being paid 60s for:

"lodemanshippe of the *Mary Rose* into the Temmys" in 1513[65]

suggesting that, at this time at least, the master was also the pilot (see above, p. 47). In May 1514, John Wodlas (or Woodeles) seems to have been her master[66] whilst, by the August of that year, the master was John Browne[67]. A number of pursers of the *Mary Rose* are also named. In October 1511, there is a record of a purser known as David Boner being paid for decking and rigging[68]. In January 1512, the purser was John Lawden[69] while, from 1513–1514, the officer was John Brereley[70]. Various captains are mentioned in association with the *Mary Rose* during these years and, in the record of expenses for the first French war of 1512–1513, Robert Sympson is named as the ship's surgeon, assisted by Henry Yonge[71]. Henry Yonge cannot still have been the surgeon when the ship sank in 1545 however since, according to the records of The Worshipful

Company of Barbers, he was still alive in 1554[72]. Given the amount of evidence for the identity of the ship's officers when the *Mary Rose* was new, and for the first French war, it seemed possible that there would be further evidence for the 1540's and, particularly, for 1545 when she sank. Initial searches uncovered no names for officers other than the Vice Admiral and the captain, however, although other officers had clearly existed. Where, then, might they be recorded?

The Letters and Papers, Foreign and Domestic of the Reign of Henry VIII which had proved such a useful source for the earlier part of the reign seemed to have no relevant information for the 1540's, so I obviously had to attempt to find other sources. Acting upon the advice of a naval historian[73], I investigated two classes in the Public Record Office, E101 and E404, for the possible names of officers, including the surgeon. There was nothing. The problem is twofold. In the first place, there are very few surviving records relating to Henry VIII's navy[74] and, secondly, the survival of what records there are is erratic, providing a discontinuous and often elusive narrative. Even the National Maritime Museum has no relevant sources in its manuscript collection[75], although the suggestion was made that the National Register of Archives might contain some information. Again, there were no records[76]. It seemed extraordinary that there was no information at all concerning the identity of either the master or the surgeon of the *Mary Rose* in 1545. Since the Company of Barbers and Surgeons was formed in 1540, perhaps The Worshipful Company of Barbers (the modern descendant of that Company) might have a record of the surgeon in 1545. When I asked, however, I found that his identity:

"has always been a mystery despite our continuous efforts to discover who he was"[72].

Apparently, although the Company did provide naval surgeons, its records do not begin until 1551. It seemed that there was nothing to be learned from the obvious lines of enquiry. The identities of the officers of the *Mary Rose* remained a mystery and I decided to explore another avenue, that of surviving wills.

It seems likely that the ship was probably crewed by men from a large area and a wide variety of backgrounds (see p. 56) and there may even have been foreign nationals among the group. Given that both Carew and Grenville were West Country men, and that they may have brought their own retinues to serve with them on the ship, I decided that the next step should be to try and find any extant West country wills that might relate to crew members.

At the beginning of World War Two, a number of maritime documents, including wills, had been removed from North Devon, particularly Barnstaple, to Exeter for safe keeping in the Probate Office[77]. At 2 a.m. on the 4th of May 1942, the Probate Office was bombed in the blitzing of Exeter and all the records it contained were destroyed[78]. The only surviving wills for that area during the period 1545–46 are a relatively small number that were collected by a Miss Olive Moger from 1921–1941[79]. There is no record of any ex-crew member of the *Mary Rose*. Other investigations in the same area, at Hartland Abbey, had a similar result[80].

It seemed that all attempts to find other members of the ship's crew, particularly the officers, had failed: there is no record of the master, the purser or the surgeon from the *Mary Rose* in 1545. By this time it had also become obvious that the only men to appear in the records would be the sons of gentry or at least the sons of those with money and position. It is clear that individual soldiers or mariners would not be named. All that is available is:

"The number and wages of the soldiers and names of those by whom they were furnished" and "the number and wages of the mariners . . . the number and wages of the gunners and monthly reward to gunners"[81].

However, one further name had emerged during the investigation.

It has been stated that, as well as Sir George Carew and Roger Grenville, the name of "a certain John Reade " is also known from the crew of 1545[82]. This John Read appears in the Additional Pedigrees of a Visitation of Buckinghamshire in 1634. Under "Read of Ludgershall, Visitation 1566" is the following:

"John Read twinne with his brother Thomas was drowned in ye *Mary Rose* at Portsmouth anno [4 of] H.8 [1512–13]"[83].

This seems to be the only reference to the incident and nothing further is known. What, one wonders, did happen to John Read? It seems that he did drown in the *Mary Rose*, although in 1512–13 and not in 1545. Because the *Mary Rose* was a new ship in 1512–13, it is unlikely that there was any incident involving her seaworthiness. Since John Read was a gentleman (hence the pedigree), perhaps he was involved in a supervisory role with the fitting-out of the ship, and somehow managed to fall off. It has been suggested that the *Mary Rose* was not in Portsmouth in 1512–13[84]. It is a matter of record, however, that she was in fact in Portsmouth on the 8th June 1513, and it seems probable that John Read was drowned at that time[85].

It is clear that there are only two named individuals from the ship – the Vice Admiral, Sir George Carew and her captain, Roger Grenville. While we know a little about these two individuals, we know nothing at all about any other crew members. Surprising as it may seem, both the master and the surgeon of the ship on 19th July 1545 are unknown, together with more than 400 other officers and men. The only evidence available about these men is that from their surviving skeletal remains. This makes the study of these remains of unique importance to the historical and archaeological records. The next three chapters will describe and discuss this study.

NOTES

1. Scammell: *Manning the English Merchant Service in the Sixteenth century*, p. 144.
2. Oxford Companion to Ships and the Sea, p. 6.
3. Wood, *MM*, 5, p. 58.
4. Whitlock, *MM*, 71, p. 168.
5. Andrew Elkerton, personal communication, 1999.
6. Grant. p. 7.
7. Rodger, p. 299; Scammell: *War at Sea under the Early Tudors*, p. 190.
8. Scammell: *Ship Owning in England 1450–1550*, p. 121.
9. Rodger, p. 299.
10. Rodger, pp. 304–5.
11. Scammell, *Manning*, p. 151.
12. Richards, p. 95.
13. Andrews, p. 259; Scammell *op. cit.*
14. Richards, *op. cit.*
15. Rodger, p. 308.
16. Scammell, *Manning*, pp. 147, 150
17. *Op. cit.*, p. 297.
18. MRT 3, p. 31.
19. Watt, *MM* 69, p. 3.
20. Watt, 1983, pp. 5–6; Gosse, p. 320.

21. Exchequer Accounts, 56 (10), 1513, referred to in Watt, p. 18.
22. Watt, 1983, p. 5–6.
23. Hildred, p. 62.
24. Rule, p. 192.
25. L&P, 20, ii); 13: Suffolk, Lisle and St. John to Henry VIII
26. Rule, p. 27.
27. Opp, p. 56.
28. Loades, p. 133.
29. Mckee, *MM* 72, p. 74.
30. Scammell: *Manning*, p. 131.
31. Opp., p. 80.
32. Rodger, p. 312.
33. Rule, p. 27.
34. Loades, p. 98, footnote no 2.
35. Keevil, pp. 62–3.
36. Rodger, p. 316.
37. Frank Green, personal communication, 2000.
38. Scammell: *War at Sea*, pp. 73 *et seq.*
39. Spont, p. 121.
40. L&P 1, i), 1132, and 1453, iii.
41. L&P 19, ii), 674.
42. Rodger, p. 314.
43. Scammell: *War at Sea*, p. 89.
44. Opp., p. 87.
45. Youings and Cornford, p. 103.
46. Scammell: *Manning*, p. 133. Rodger also says that: "Most ships had one or two boys but not more", p. 320.
47. Youings and Cornford, p 103; Scammell: *Manning*, p. 138.
48. Scammell: *Manning*, p. 139.
49. L&P 20, i), 59 and 106.
50. Rowse, p. 249.
51. L&P 20, i), 192, 217 and 1263.
52. Rodger, p. 319.
53. Andrews, p. 257.
54. Goodman, *MM* 60, pp. 28–9.
55. Rodger, p. 320.
56. Andrews, p. 148.
57. Scammell, *Manning*, pp. 147–50.
58. *Op. cit.*, p. 135.
59. *Op. cit.*, p. 136; Rodger, p. 324.
60. Hair and Alsop, pp. 87–8.
61. Hildred, p. 65.
62. L&P 1, ii), 3608.

63. *Op. cit.*, John Daunce's accounts.
64. *Op. cit.*, January 28th, and number 1661, Exchequer Accounts 62 (15) R.O. Navy Records Society X, 77.
65. *Op. cit.*, 3608.
66. *Op. cit.*, 2865.
67. *Op. cit.*, 5721 (2), 6.
68. *Op. cit.*, 3608, October 18th.
69. *Op. cit.*, January 28th.
70. L&P 1, i), 2305 iii, and 1, ii), 5721 (2), 6.
71. L&P 1, ii), 3614, Exchequer Accounts 56 (10) R.O. 1514-15, War Expenses.
72. I. G. Murray, personal communication, 1998.
73. N. A. M. Rodger, personal communication, 1998.
74. A. Hawkyard, personal communication, 1999.
75. C. Powell, personal communication, 1998.
76. I. Hart, personal communication, 1998.
77. Barnstaple Museum, personal communication, 1998.
78. Public records relating to the blitzing of Exeter in May, 1942, West Country Studies Library, Exeter.
79. Wills and other Records, Vol. III (Bremel-Cawley).
80. Sir Hugh Stucley, personal communication, 1998.
81. L&P 1, i), 1661, 4 (4377).
82. MRT 3, p. 28.
83. Publications of the Harleian Society, Vol. LVIII; MDCCCCIX (1909).
84. Margaret Rule, personal communication, 1999.
85. L&P Vol 1, ii) 2305 ii (162–5) Naval Payments.

SIX

The Skeleton Crew of the Mary Rose: Basic Data

THE NATURE OF THE REMAINS

When the *Mary Rose* heeled over and sank in July, 1545, she came to rest on her starboard side, at an angle of 60° from the vertical (see chapter 2). The sinking was so rapid that only about 35 men escaped drowning. From the Cowdray engraving, these men appear to have been in the fighting tops (figure 1); the anti-boarding netting covering all exposed decks trapped the rest. There are four tides a day in the Solent, providing strong currents which run both in an east/west direction and, less strongly, from north-east to south-west. The *Mary Rose* lay broadside to these currents[1], which not only deposited silts within the ship but also eroded a deep, wide scourpit on the port side and a small, narrow scourpit on the starboard side of the hull (figure 2a). While the starboard scourpit quickly filled with silts, the port one stayed open for much longer, allowing this exposed side of the ship to become weakened and abraded by the currents[1]. This side finally collapsed downwards into the wreck and the scourpits (figure 2b). A hard, shelly seabed was laid down in the late seventeenth or the early eighteenth century, sealing all the Tudor levels in the wreck. A much more mobile seabed formed later above this (figure 2c) which periodically, because of its mobility, was wholly or partially removed. So, the wreck became partially exposed from time to time, allowing for its eventual discovery. The speed of the sinking and the angle at which the ship came to rest caused it to become deeply embedded in the seabed clays. Some of the heavier objects on board plunged across from the tilting port side and into the ship as she heeled and, during the following weeks and months as she silted up, lighter objects were moved around by the water within the hull, causing mixing and further damage[2]. Clearly, the site would present problems of excavation for the archaeologists. Neither had any comparable ship been excavated. The *Vasa*, for example, had sunk in very different circumstances and was resting in a horizontal position. Both the amount of mixing and of damage to material within the ship were unknown for the *Mary Rose*. How were these problems to be tackled?

The wreck-site lay in an area of effluence only about a kilometer offshore and the underwater visibility was poor. So, a three-metre grid of highly visible yellow-painted metal pole-work was erected horizontally above the site, dividing it into a number of trenches[3], (figure 10). These trenches were numbered 1 – 11 sequentially from bow to stern and excavated a layer at a time. A diver's working area was about 1 meter square, although this could vary according to working conditions and the size or shape of an individual object[4]. All found objects were recorded by their positions within the hull in sectors, by reference both to the trenches and to the decks. Thus, H4 was the sector in trench 4 between the hold and the orlop deck above, whilst O4 was the sector in the same trench, but between the orlop and the main deck (figure 11). The ship gradually became exposed using this system and was finally lifted, as described in chapter 1.

Men had been trapped at all levels in the ship during the sinking, but, understandably, had tended to congregate in areas where there were companionways (figure 7). The angle at which the ship lay, the movement of water within the wreck and the action of marine predators, who removed parts of decomposing bodies, all led to mixing of the human remains. This mixing was further complicated by movement and damage to the decks in some areas of the ship, for example between the sectors 7 and 8 of the hold and orlop decks. When human bone was encountered in the wreck during the excavation, this mixing was very apparent (Plate 1) so the remains were excavated by sector, just as they were found (Plate 2). They were recorded and raised to the surface for conservation and specialist study. After they came ashore, groups of bones which had been found together were given the same number and put into netting bags; skulls and jaws (mandibles) were kept separate. Next, the nets of bones were washed for four weeks in a cascade of

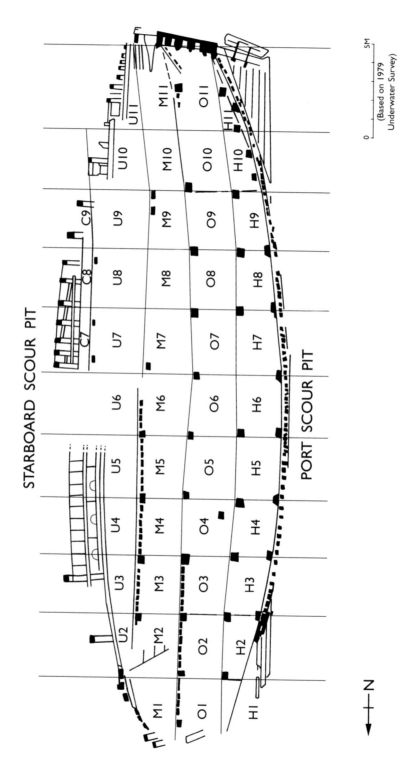

Figure 10. Flat plan of the wreck, showing the trench excavation grid and sectors. Copyright © the Mary Rose Trust.

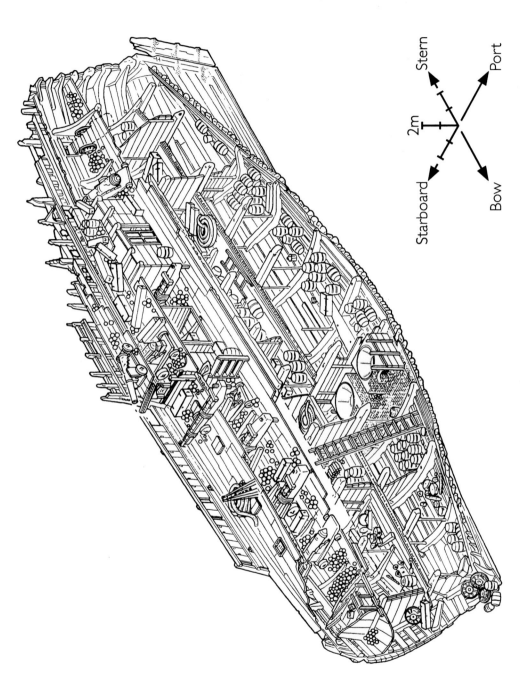

Stern

Port

2m

Starboard

Bow

Figure 11. Isometric projection showing the wreck with stowage and some damaged areas. Copyright © the Mary Rose Trust.

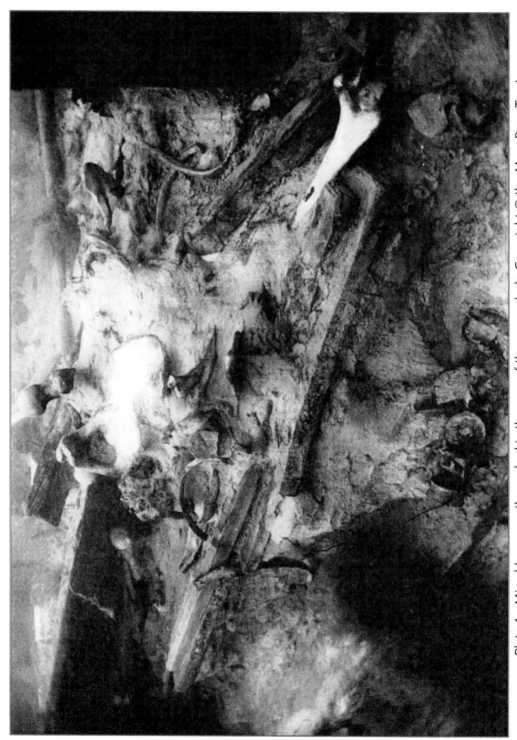

Plate 1. Mixed bones on the seabed in the area of the upper deck. Copyright © the Mary Rose Trust.

Plate 2. Remains of a possible archer on the seabed; note the spacer of arrows below the scale. Copyright © the Mary Rose Trust.

clean, fresh water, running through four baths. Each group of nets started in the bottom bath, moving up the cascade a week at a time. Finally, the bones were dried and individually numbered. I received all the excavated human remains in 1984, apart from three skulls which had gone to Bristol for CT scanning, and which were sent to me later[5]. The bones arrived in groups in their nets, most of them packed into very large boxes. The skulls and mandibles were in separate, small boxes and some of the unassociated femurs were in other, long boxes. Needless to say, they were all still completely mixed (Plate 3). Given the unique nature of the group and the site, however, I decided to try and sort them into individuals.

The anaerobic conditions of the seabed silts, in which there was no free oxygen, had slowed down the processes of decomposition, so that the preservation of the majority of organic material from the ship, including the human bone, was superb. A small amount of bone, which had become exposed on the seabed, was eroded and some was heavily stained with iron oxides but, generally, the surviving human skeletal remains were in an excellent condition. The bone appeared to be, and was, hard and robust with unusually clear markings at the areas of muscle attachments (Plate 4). There seemed to be a reasonable possibility that at least some of the bones might be matched with others to make up single individuals.

There are 206 bones in the human skeleton[6]. Specific bones will be discussed later but, in terms of the mixing of the burials and the task of sorting the bones into individuals, it was obvious that I should start with those bones that occur in pairs. These include the three bones from each arm, the four bones from each leg, the pelvic bones, shoulder blades, collar bones and those of the hands and feet. When they are well preserved, the larger of these bones can often be matched into pairs: the hands and feet are more difficult.

Given the number of bones in the human skeleton and the amount of mixing in the wreck, the prospect of attempting to derive complete individuals from the large mass of excavated bone was rather intimidating. I was very lucky, however, to have the help of two excellent students over the period of a year for the sorting and recording work[7]. It was decided first to take all the bone from each sector of the ship separately and see whether any matching could be achieved. There were variable amounts of bone in each sector. For example, there were large groups of bones in areas where there had been companionways, such as in H4. This was also the case where areas of deck had been damaged or had moved (Plate 3) so sorting of these remains was very time consuming. We started with the femur (Plate 4). Having matched pairs of femurs, we proceeded down the leg, matching the tibia of the shin and the accompanying fibula into pairs (figure 12): the paired femurs were then matched, at the knee, with the tibias. Next, we put the sides of the pelvis together where we could, and fitted the matching femurs into the hip joints. Having got this far, we decided to try and assemble the spinal columns: this proved easier than we had anticipated, since the 32 bones of the spine do fit together quite snugly. If we were fortunate enough to have a sacrum from the base of the spine (figure 12), we could sit the column on top of this, starting with the 5th lumbar vertebra. If we had the first cervical vertebra of the neck, we could then fit the skull on to that. (The mandibles were sorted and fitted to skulls by a team from Birmingham Dental School and this work will be discussed later). So far, we had the legs, pelvis, spine and head of an individual. Arms, shoulder blades, collar bones, kneecaps, hands and feet were also sorted into pairs but these could not be added to an individual skeleton, because of the

Plate 3.   The commingled burials from the area of the orlop
and hold decks, sectors 7 and 8.

form of their joints. While the hip joint is a 'ball and socket', the head of the femur fitting snugly into the hip joint, the shoulder joint is different. It is made up of three loosely associated bones, the humerus, shoulder blade (scapula) and collar bone (clavicle, figure 12). The articulation of these bones largely depends on the supporting soft tissue, the ligaments, tendons and muscles, which allows the arm to be swung in any direction and to be rotated through 360°. There is no snug socket into which the joint fits as there is for the hip. The wrist and ankle joints have a similar articulation to the shoulder and cannot be closely associated with the arm or the leg. So, because of their structures, neither the shoulder, the wrist nor the ankle joints can be fitted together accurately in dry bone. Neither can groups of ribs be fitted to the breastbone (sternum, figure 12) in an individual skeleton. Equally, the kneecap (patella) is 'floating' and has no fixed association with the other leg bones at the knee. Therefore, shoulders, hands and feet, ribs, breastbone and kneecaps were not included with an individual unless there was a clear archaeological association between them on the seabed.

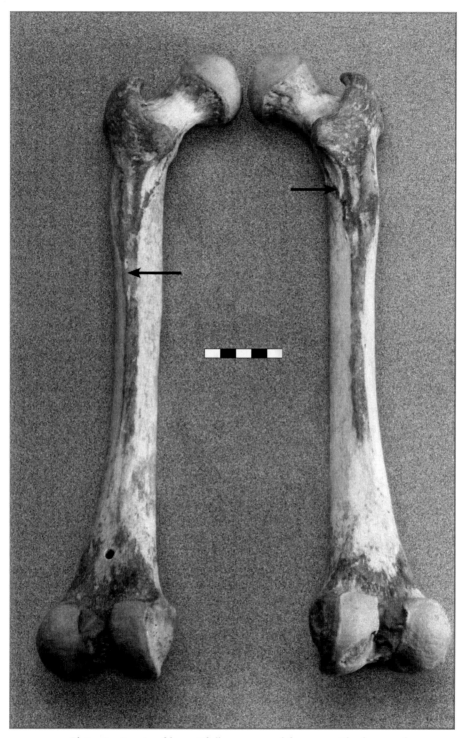

Plate 4. A pair of beautifully preserved femurs with clear and
prominent muscle insertions (arrows).

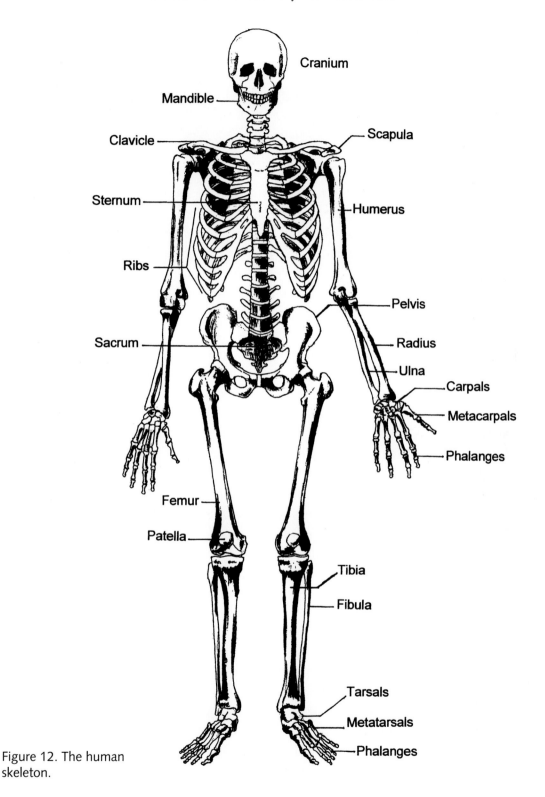

Figure 12. The human skeleton.

The result of all the sorting and recording work was that a total of 92 Fairly Complete Skeletons were derived from the mass of human skeletal remains from the *Mary Rose*, some of which were more complete than others. Some of the bones making up a single individual came from more than one sector of the ship and this was recorded. There were a few cases where an individual had obviously been trapped under or close to a very large or heavy object, such as a bronze gun, and had stayed in place until found and excavated. There were other cases, for example down in the hold, where men did not appear to have moved far from where they had died. These individuals were some of the most complete in the group. The rest of the mixed and unmatched human material was recorded by bone and by sector.

DETERMINING NUMBERS OF INDIVIDUAL MEN

In order to calculate the number of individuals in a mixed group of skeletons, it is necessary to count both the numbers of the most frequently occurring individual bones such as the skull, and of the paired bones, such as those of the arms and legs. Estimating these numbers from the *Mary Rose* was obviously made even more difficult because of the mixing of the burials by the sea. However, the fine quality of the surviving bone enabled us to pair many bones, as just described. Since each of us has only one skull and jawbone, and only one left or right arm or leg, the maximum surviving number of any of these bones would give the minimum number of individuals present. The team from the University of Birmingham Dental School matched the skulls and mandibles. The results of this work emphasised the amount of mixing. In one case, for example, a skull from one deck was matched with its jawbone from three decks below. So, the archaeological boundaries were not necessarily useful as indicators of individual placement and, therefore, the skulls and mandibles were matched across the entire ship. The results of this matching are shown in Table 1. The totals for bones which occur in pairs are shown in Table 2.

From Table 2, the minimum number of individuals based on the left humerus count is 119. From Table 1, however, the minimum number based on the skull and mandible count is 179. If the crew size was 415 men on the day she sank, 179 represents about 43 per cent of that crew. Since the burials were excavated from roughly half the ship (figure 13), this figure is probably

Table 1: Numbers of skulls and mandibles

Matched skulls with mandibles	68
Unmatched skulls	58
Unmatched mandibles	48
Matched maxillas with mandibles	2
Skulls from Bristol	3
TOTALS	179

Table 2: Total numbers of bones occurring in pairs

	Left	Right
Pelvis	107	108
Femur	114	110
Tibia	108	117
Fibula	105	96
Scapula	102	105
Clavicle	84	90
Humerus	119*	99
Radius**	107	98
Ulna**	105	92
TOTALS	951	915

*Highest individual score;
** There are 2 radii and 2 ulnas which were broken and could not be given a side. These have not been included in the totals.
(Note: The above are bones which always occur in pairs in the human body. However, in Table 2, they have been counted for each side wherever they occurred in the sample: they were not necessarily in pairs, hence the discrepancy in the numbers for each side).

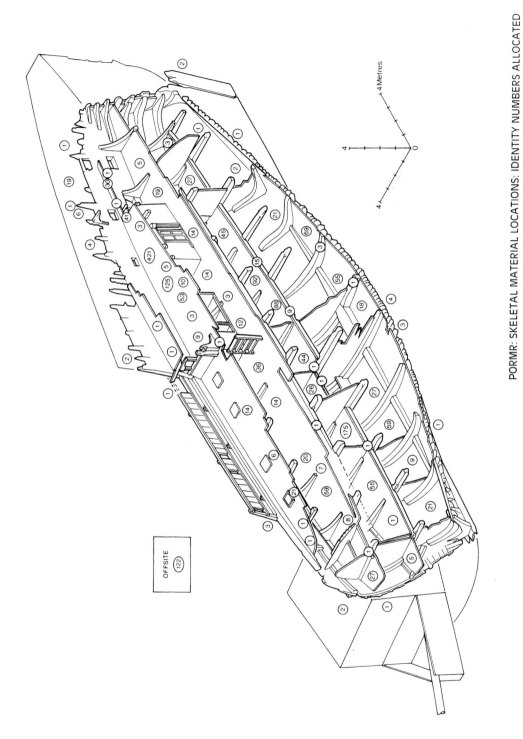

PORMR: SKELETAL MATERIAL LOCATIONS: IDENTITY NUMBERS ALLOCATED

Figure 13. Isometric projection of the wreck, showing the general distribution of the human skeletal remains and the numbers of individual bones found in each area. Copyright ©, the Mary Rose Trust.

fairly accurate. There is, however, the apocryphal tale that there were an extra 300 men – probably archers – on board the ship when she sank, although there is no firm evidence for this figure. It is said to have come from the brother of a crew member who saw the ship sinking. (See Chapter 1, reference 7 and Chapter 2, reference 53). If this figure were true, it would make the ship's complement 715 men and change our sample size to 25 per cent. When she sank, however, the anti-boarding netting trapped the majority of men and it seems likely that, had there been an extra 300 on board, the excavation would have found many more human skeletal remains. Therefore, a crew of 415 and a sample of 43 per cent seem more reasonable figures than a crew of 715 and a sample of 25 per cent. Whatever the true figure, the rest of the men are either still buried at the site or have drifted away from the wreck.

DETERMINING SEX AND AGE AT DEATH

The sex of an individual skeleton can only be identified if a) that individual was an adolescent or an adult and b) the relevant bones are present. It is not possible to sex the skeletons of children using our present techniques, although some new work does suggest the possibility of sexing children's skeletons by using DNA[8]. The differences between the sexes, which we see in the living, are also present to some degree in the skeleton. Certain bones show the strongest sexual differences; these are the skull and the pelvis, particularly the pelvis. Since it has to cope with both pregnancy and childbirth, the female pelvis is constructed differently from the male and is both shallower and broader[9]. On the other hand, generally the male skull and jaw are heavier and larger than the female, with stronger and more developed areas of muscle attachment. This is particularly noticeable at the back of the skull, where the neck muscles attach to the bone, on the chin and at the angle of the jaw[10]. As well as these major sexual differences in the skeleton, there are other skeletal differences between the sexes. These include measurements of the joints of the humerus and femur, particularly their heads, and the lengths of the collar bones. Men generally have larger and longer bones than women. Measurements of the heads of the femur and humerus and of the length of the collarbone were used to sex unassociated long bones from the ship[11]. The Fairly Complete Skeletons were sexed using all the bones present for each individual.

There are five categories used to sex human skeletal remains. They are:

F (female); ?F (probable female); ? (undetermined); ?M (probable male); M (male)

When they were used for the burials from the *Mary Rose*, every skeleton was that of a male or probable male. This is perhaps not surprising on a warship. If it was the custom to have women on board these ships while they were in port, there were none amongst the skeletal material that I examined.

Unlike sexing, the age at death of an individual is easier to determine for juveniles, adolescents and young adults in their twenties than it is for older individuals. There are two different methods, each of which gives reasonably precise ages. The first involves identifying the pattern of eruption and the state of root formation of the deciduous and the permanent teeth. The second involves examination of the state of closure of the *epiphyses*. The *epiphyses* are the growing ends of long bones or of flat bones, which are joined to the bone by a plate of cartilage. This allows the main part of the bone to continue growing. The ends join to the shafts or main bones as the adolescent stops growing (see Appendix I)[12]. Usually, all the permanent teeth have erupted and growth has finished in both sexes by the age of 25 or thereabouts. After this, the estimation of age becomes more difficult.

Traditionally, the patterns of wear on the permanent molar teeth have been used to estimate the age at death of adults[13], but this method does have its problems. Wear patterns were originally assessed for two separate groups: pre-medieval British and Anglo-Saxon skeletons. Both these groups are distant in time and it is difficult to know much about their diet and life-styles. These factors would affect the wear patterns on their teeth and, therefore, the ages that were estimated from them. This being so, it is difficult to apply the same criteria, with confidence in their accuracy, to other skeletal groups from later time periods. There is a further problem. It is, apparently, impossible to assess the age of individual adults from tooth wear if there are no infants and children in the group (based on tooth eruption) to provide the necessary baseline information[14]. So, while tooth wear patterns gave us some indication of the ages of the crew, they were not used for specific individual ages.

Changes associated with ageing also occur in other parts of the skeleton. They include alterations at the pubic symphysis, where the two halves of the pelvis meet at the front[15], and changes that happen at the rib ends, particularly where they join the breastbone[16].

There were problems in trying to age individuals in these burials, due to the amount of mixing of the bones. It would clearly be possible to count an individual more than once, especially as parts of his skeleton may have been in different sectors of the ship. So, it was obvious that only the 92 Fairly Complete Skeletons (FCS) could be aged with any confidence since these had been uniquely matched. All possible ageing techniques and criteria were used to age these 92 FCS's. These produced a large number of age categories or ranges so it was necessary then to simplify these.

Traditionally, ages of individual adults have been presented as belonging within a specific range, for example, 18–25 years, 25–35 years and so on. Practically, however, the numerical results from using the various ageing methods often give widely differing values, which it is not possible to fit into such tight age ranges. We have also probably tended to over-age younger individuals and under-age older ones[8, 17]. In addition to this, recent work on the burials from the crypt of Christ Church at Spitalifelds in London has emphasised the point, where:

"Our findings have affirmed (sic) our fears that traditional methods of determining age at death are inaccurate"[18].

Table 3: Numbers of individuals in each age category

Juveniles = 1*	Middle-aged adults = 15
Adolescents = 17	Old adults = 1**
Young adults = 54	

TOTAL = 88

* There is probably more than one child. The FCS juvenile is about 12 –13 years of age, but there were other bones (not in the FCS group) with unfused epiphyses suggesting a child of only about 10 years.
** There were some non-FCS odd bones with a degree of osteoarthritis which could have belonged to other old adult individuals in the group.
Note: 4 FCS's could only be aged as 'adult' and have, therefore, not been included.

Given all the problems of ageing adults, the FCS's from the *Mary Rose* have, therefore, been placed in three categories, those of Young, Middle or Old adults:

1. Young Adults are aged from about 18 to about 30 years
2. Middle Adults from about 30 to about 40 years
3. Old Adults are over 40 years

There are also a small number of juveniles (pre-adolescents) and some adolescents (under about 18 years) in the FCS group.

The results are shown in Table 3 and are probably fairly predictable for such a group.

DETERMINING STATURE AND VARIOUS SKELETAL INDICES

Stature

It is possible to calculate the height of an individual adult skeleton. This can be done using the lengths of various long bones and applying regression equations formulated in 1970 for American burials[19]. The best results (with the smallest standard deviation) were achieved by using a combination of the maximum lengths of the femur and the tibia[19]. There seemed to be a greater accuracy when the leg bones rather than the arm bones were used. More recent work has shown that the best estimate of height for British skeletal material, at least for males, is achieved by using the femur only, rather than any other long bone of the skeleton[20]. The heights of the *Mary Rose* men were estimated using their left femurs, following this later work. Only the left femurs were used, so that the same man was not measured twice. Using only one bone also avoided any problems associated with the possible mixing of skeletons.

Trotter's formula and the tabulated height for the *Mary Rose* men are given in Appendix II. The statures ranged from 159cm (5' 3") to 180cm (5' 11") with a mean of 171cm (5' 7"). The standard deviation (SD) is between 4 and 5 cm or about 2", so about 68 per cent or just over two thirds of the heights will have been within +/- 1 SD of the mean. How does this compare with other groups?

One of the commonest assumptions made about people in the past is that they were considerably shorter than modern groups. Most of the historical information on adult males is obtained from military conscription, while earlier data come from archaeological work. Comparisons with archaeology are tricky, since it is not always clear which bone was used to calculate stature, or whether the same formulae have been used throughout. There is also the problem of applying the results from relatively modern American males to European archaeological data. Nevertheless, such results as there are do provide some interesting comparisons.

Kunitz compared the heights of adult males in England from the first to the nineteenth centuries[17]. The mean heights for the first millennium are very similar to those for the end of the nineteenth century, ranging from 170cm to 174cm: clearly, the *Mary Rose* men lie within these ranges. Male height seems to have dipped markedly from the thirteenth to the early nineteenth century, a fact that Kunitz relates to social factors such as poor nutrition and patterns of health and disease[17]. Comparisons with European males of conscription age are even more interesting. The average height during the last 200 years seems to have varied between 159cm and 181cm[19]. The shortest mean height so far recorded was 159cm for 18 year old recruits to the eighteenth century Habsburg armies, while Spanish recruits in 1913 had a mean height of 164cm[21]. These military recruits would not have stopped growing, of course, so these are not their final heights. The authors suggest an addition of about three per cent for further growth, on the basis of similar modern populations in the under-developed countries, giving an estimated final mean of 165cm for the shortest men. At the higher end, the tallest recruits in Europe were 17-year olds in the Dutch army in 1982, with a mean stature of 181cm. But, modern adults are apparently achieving skeletal maturity earlier than was the case in the past. The authors therefore suggest that no more than one per cent further growth should be assumed for these modern populations, giving an estimated final mean height of not more than 183cm for the tallest men[21].

Only fully mature adult bones were measured from the *Mary Rose* remains, so that the statures calculated represent final skeletal height. If we take the estimated means of young European males for the last 200 years, the range of final heights is between about 165cm and about 183cm. The mid-point of this range is 174cm or about 5' 8½". Applying the standard deviation to the mean of the *Mary Rose* men (see Appendix II) gives a range from 165cm (5' 5") to 175cm (5' 9"), which places them very close to the European recruits. So, comparison with both the archaeological/historical material and the army conscripts places the crew comfortably within these groups as far as their height was concerned. Whilst they were not as tall as the tallest modern Dutch or Scandinavian men, they were no shorter than many of their other modern counterparts.

The Cranial Index

There are three indices which help to describe the general shape of an individual's head and face: the Cranial, Orbital and Total Facial Indices. They are based on certain measurements of the skull and face which are always taken from specific landmarks or points on the bone. The Cranial Index expresses, as a percentage, the ratio of the breadth of the skull to its length. The results are usually placed into one of four categories, so that individuals are either long headed (dolichocranic), medium headed (mesocranic), round headed (brachycranic) or very round headed (hyperbrachycranic). Both the derivations of the index and the results for the *Mary Rose* crew are given in Appendix II.

The majority of the men have a medium head shape. However, thirteen individuals are more long headed and, of these, four have very long and narrow heads. At the other end of the scale, eleven individuals are more round headed and one of these is at the extreme top end of the values, with a skull that was very inflated and round.

The Orbital Index

The Orbital Index is based on measurements of the eye socket: these are the maximum height and the maximum breadth. Three categories are use to describe the shape of the socket, so that an individual either has wide orbits (chamaeconchy), medium orbits (mesoconchy) or narrow orbits (hypsiconchy). The index is evaluated in a similar way to the Cranial Index and the results for the crew are shown in Appendix II.

The majority of the men have medium-shaped eye sockets. Five individuals, however, have rather wide sockets and eight have rather narrow ones, with one man having very narrow sockets indeed.

The Total Facial Index

The Total Facial Index expresses the ratio of the height to the breadth of the face, including the teeth; it can only be derived if both the skull and the jawbone are present and intact. Five categories are used to express the overall shape of the face, so that an individual either has a very broad face (hypereuryprosopy), a broad face (euryprosopy), a medium face (mesoprosopy), a narrow face (leptoprosopy) or an extremely narrow face (hyperleptoprosopy). The results for the present group are given in Appendix II.

The distribution for this index was rather flat, with the faces evenly spread between the broad, average and narrow groups. However, there were two faces, one at each end of the scale, which had extreme values (72.9 and 106.2). These values were probably unreliable, however, as both jaws were pathological – the lower one with extreme tooth decay and poor occlusion (matching of the jaws) and the other with a very swollen jaw on one side.

The above results show the crew to have been a group of men with heads and eyes that were generally average or medium in shape, and faces that were distributed between the broad, average and narrow shapes. In other words, they will have looked very like us and they would fit easily into the modern population.

Post-cranial Indices

There are a number of indices that describe the size and shape of other bones of the skeleton, as well as the skull. For example, the Robusticity Index describes the physique of the individual by comparing the relative sizes of the shafts of either the humerus or the femur to their individual lengths. It can be used to make comparisons between the right and left-sided bones, and between different archaeological groups.

The robusticity index was calculated for matching pairs of humeri and femurs from the *Mary Rose*. The results were compared with those from a group of males from another archaeological site, the medieval parish cemetery of St. Margaret Fyebridgegate in Magdalen Street, Norwich. There were no significant differences between the right and left sides in the femur, for either group of men. However, the results for the humerus showed that the right humerus of the men from Norwich was significantly more robust than the left, while the *Mary Rose* men showed no difference in robusticity between their arms[22]. This seems to imply that the Norwich men were tending to use their right arms more than their left while the *Mary Rose* men seem to have been using their arms more equally. Since nearly 90 per cent of us are right-handed, the right arm is used preferentially by the human species as a whole. The men from Norwich seem to be following this trend, but not the men from the *Mary Rose*. Possible reasons for this will be discussed in later chapters.

The teeth

Although I recorded all the teeth that I found when examining the human skeletal material from the *Mary Rose*, the full, comprehensive analysis of the teeth was done by the group of four dentists from Birmingham University Dental School. Some of this work has been published (in abstract form only[23]), and has been recently updated by R.I.W. Evans, one of the original workers, in a report for the Mary Rose Trust. There are some general remarks about the teeth that we can make from this work[24].

The dentists examined and reported on 143 individuals. These consisted of 68 matched skulls and mandibles and 75 matched upper (maxillae) and lower (mandibular) jaws. From these they deduced that, although the shapes of the mouths were similar, the *Mary Rose* men had better matching of the teeth between the two jaws (occlusion) than their modern counterparts. The dental arches were a good shape, compared with those today. There was a lack of crowding but much more wear (attrition), probably contributing to the lack of crowding, and implying a much coarser diet for the men than a modern one[14]. Of the 143 individuals, 119 (83 per cent) had caries, 18 (13 per cent) had abscesses and 52 (36 per cent) had ante-mortem loss of teeth, either because they had been extracted in life or because they had never erupted. The total numbers of teeth examined were 4,576 and, of these, 416 (9 per cent) had decayed teeth (carious lesions):

> 247 lesions – 59 per cent – either in occlusal fissures on the tops of the teeth or at contact points between the teeth;
> 93 lesions – 22 per cent – either below the contact points or at the junction of the root and the enamel (cemento-enamel junction);
> 76 lesions – 18 per cent – were gross[14].

The conclusions from this work are both interesting and difficult to explain. Apparently, the crew of the *Mary Rose* is the earliest known group to show a modern pattern of decay. Cavities occurred more commonly on exposed root surfaces in even earlier groups whereas, for the *Mary Rose* group, they were found more frequently on the occlusal surfaces and at the enamel contact areas between teeth, as is the case today. This pattern of decay is also similar to that found in a group dating from 1665[23]. Although there was no widespread consumption of sugar in the first half of the sixteenth century, it has been suggested that the crew probably used honey "and other cariogenic foods and drinks"[14]. There is no archaeological evidence for the use of honey at this time and such victualling evidence as there is makes no mention of honey (see Chapter 4). It is not unreasonable to assume, however, that some honey was consumed, although whether this and other such foods were consumed in sufficient quantity to lead to the levels of decay seen in the crew is another matter. Whatever the causes of the problem, Evans suggests that at least 10 per cent of the crew could have been in dental pain at any one time[14].

Having studied the human skeletal remains of the crew of the *Mary Rose*, what physical picture of them emerges? The members of the *Mary Rose* crew were a group of predominantly young men in their late teens and twenties. Their average height was about 5' 7" and their facial appearance was similar to ours, with largely medium-shaped heads. Their eyes and faces, like ours, varied between the broad, medium and narrow shapes, and they will probably have had more visible scars than most modern young men. Their dental condition was fairly good, with arches that were a good shape, and their occlusion was better then ours with less crowding. This was probably due to a coarser diet. It is interesting that while their pattern of tooth decay was similar to ours, the reasons for this are unclear. They were strong and robust and seem to have been using their arms more equally than was the case with a comparable group. This idea will be explored in later chapters.

NOTES

1. Rule, p. 44
2. See, for example, p. 87 and figure 1 of Richards.
3. Rule, pp. 78, 79.
4. Andrew Elkerton, personal communication, 2000.
5. It was thought that these three skulls might still contain some brain matter, hence the CT scanning at Bristol University.
6. Generally, this is the correct number, but there are variations. For example, some people have one more or one less vertebra than usual and others have small accessory bones in the hands and feet.
7. Both were archaeology students who went on to work with human bone. Jacqui Bowman came for the summer vacation from Leicester University to work with me at the beginning of the study and Christine Osborne came from Bradford University on a year's placement to complete the work.
8. Stone *et al.* 1996.
9. See Stirland, 1999, p. 28 and figure 14 for an extended discussion of this. Also Aiello and Dean, figure 20.16.

10. Stirland, 1999, figure 15.
11. Krogman, 1978; Ubelaker, 1984, pp. 41–4.
12. Stirland, 1999, pp. 30–2.
13. Brothwell, 1981; Miles, 1963.
14. R. I. W. Evans, personal communication, 1998.
15. Suchey *et al.* 1988.
16. Işcan *et al.* 1984, p. 85.
17. Kunitz, p. 271, Table 1.
18. Molleson and Cox, p. 214.
19. Trotter, p. 77, Table XXVIII; Harrison *et al.*, p. 301 *et seq.*
20. Waldron, p 76.
21. Floud *et al.*, p. 22
22. Stirland, 1992, p. 127, Table 5.5.2.
23. Corbett and Anderson, p. 968.
24. For anyone interested in the details of the dentitions from the *Mary Rose*, Evans's work will be included in the forthcoming report on the human skeletal remains, to be produced by the Mary Rose Trust.

SEVEN

The Skeleton Crew of the Mary Rose: *General Pathology*

The human skeleton is a collection of bones held together by connective tissue (ligaments). Bone is a living entity, plastic in nature and constantly changing: we have a new skeleton approximately every ten years. The ability of bone to change is obvious from the way it grows and also from its response to any attack on it caused by disease, by accident or even by patterns of activity. Some, but not all, of these insults will leave a permanent record on the skeleton. For example, long-term destructive diseases, such as leprosy and tuberculosis, can produce characteristic bone lesions, whereas sudden non-violent death doesn't affect the skeleton. On the other hand, violent individual attack by axe, sword or gun will leave evidence on the bones, either of survival, because the bones have healed and remodelled or of death, because they have not.

When studying an archaeological group of skeletons it is unusual for the cause of death to be known, but it is a matter of record that most of the crew of the *Mary Rose* died by drowning. The manner of their death has left no record on their bones, but other conditions have done so. These include evidence for some diseases as discussed below.

DISEASES OF MALNUTRITION

It has been shown by considering the evidence for victualling (see Chapter 4) that the diet of the sixteenth century mariner was restricted, although it may have been better than that of the majority of agricultural workers (see Chapter 3). There are degrees of dietary deficiency, ranging from total starvation on the one hand to a lack of some essential nutrients on the other. Any imbalance in diet, including excess, can result in a disease. If prolonged, a lack of essential nutrients may lead to well-recognised deficiency diseases that can effect the skeleton, although the accurate recognition and recording of such effects can be difficult.

Vitamin D, (which is responsible for the absorption of calcium and phosphorus and the formation of bone) can be obtained from eating fish oils and animal fats such as cheese and butter. However, its main source is the action of the ultraviolet rays of sunlight on dehydrocholesterol in the skin[1]. In children, a lack of vitamin D can lead to the deficiency disease known as rickets. This lack of vitamin D results in bones that are 'soft' or incompletely mineralized and, when an infant is crawling with his weight on his arms or walking with his weight on his legs, the loading on the 'softened' long bones of the arms or legs causes them to bend. Thus, the effect of rickets on the growing child's skeleton is to deform the weight-bearing bones[2], and these bending deformities can persist into adult life.

The adult form of rickets is osteomalacia which is caused, like rickets, by a deficiency of vitamin D. There is also a deficiency of protein and fat in this condition together with a low intake, or a loss through intestinal disease, of calcium and phosphorus[3]. The skeleton becomes demineralized, resulting in collapse and deformity of the ribs, breastbone, spine and pelvis under load-bearing stresses. Because the long bones are fully formed in the adult they are not usually affected.

There are probable examples of both healed childhood rickets and adult osteomalacia in the men from the *Mary Rose*. Two femurs are bowed from front to back (Plate 5) and twelve tibias are bowed from side to side (Plate 6). All these bones have the appearance of healed childhood rickets. Osteomalacia is implied by one fused, expanded and very bowed breastbone (sternum, Plate 7a) and two very angulated sacrums from the base of the spine, one of which is shown in Plate 8. All these bones give the impression that some members of the crew suffered dietary deficiencies when they were children and some when they were adults.

A prolonged deficiency in vitamin C (ascorbic acid) causes scurvy, a disease mainly affecting the connective tissues of the body, causing haemorrhage in many areas. It does not produce the distinctive and characteristic bone changes of rickets or osteomalacia, athough some

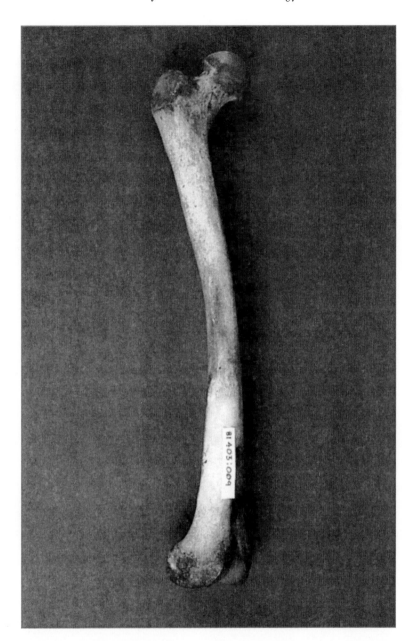

Plate 5. A bowed
femur: healed
childhood rickets.

skeletal changes do occur, especially in the very young. It is a difficult
disease to diagnose in dry bone. As well as causing extensive bleeding,
scurvy also reduces the body's resistance to infection[4]. Therefore, it can
occur in association with outbreaks of dysentery or tropical sprue, and
often did so on the long exploratory sea voyages of the past[5]. Scurvy can
affect many organs and, if left untreated, can kill. It has been recognised
as a serious disease for many years, the signs of which were referred to as

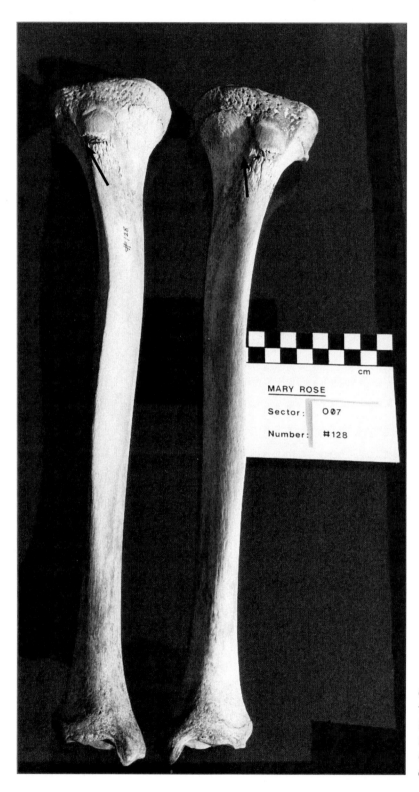

6. Bowed tibias: the top part of the bones is bowed mediolaterally (arrows). Healed childhood rickets.

7 a). Fused, bowed sternum: osteomalacia. b) Normal sternum for comparison.

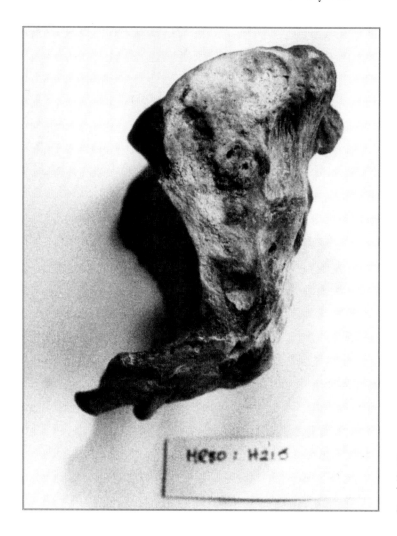

Plate 8. Angulated sacrum: osteomalacia. The normal sacrum has a gentle curve only.

early as 1541[6]. Although James Lind, the Scottish naval surgeon, pioneered work on treatment of the disease in the eighteenth century, his ideas were not initially adopted. In "A Treatise of the Scurvy", which he published in 1753, Lind recommended a daily issue of lemon juice to sailors to prevent scurvy, having already shown that patients with the disease recovered when treated with the juice[7]. Nevertheless, thousands of seamen died before his work was generally accepted and anti-scorbutic agents were incorporated into their diets. A diet that is low in fresh fruit and vegetables, or one that consists largely of cooked food (boiling destroys vitamin C), will cause the disease to appear in individuals and in populations. Scorbutic bleeding occurs in the skin, the gums and the periosteum (the living membrane which surrounds all bones, other than the joint capsules and surfaces). Its affects are particularly clear on the bones of young children, where the results of chronic haemorrhaging into the periosteum, particularly of the arm and leg bones, are the most important single sign of scurvy[8]. In the healing phase of the disease, the resulting blood clots (haematomas) ossifiy or calcify, producing 'lumpy' new bone along the shafts. This can sometimes be seen in archaeological skeletons. Recent work suggests that, in children, this chronic bleeding also occurs at multiple sites on the skull[9], causing an abnormal pitting (porosity) of the surface. The eye sockets (orbits) and areas of muscle-attachment on the skull that are associated with chewing seem to be particularly affected[10]. Some changes may also occur in adults, including bleeding into the joints and the gums and, possibly, some splitting

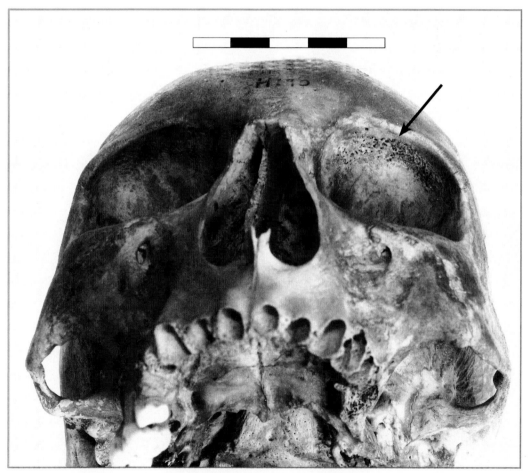

Plate 9. Possible healed, adolescent scurvy. New bone appears to be on top of the old in the top of these eye sockets (arrow).

of bone longitudinally[11], as well as haemorrhages along the long bone shafts[12]. Scurvy was, and is, the scourge of people exposed to war and to famine. Displaced and dispossessed people may, of course, suffer from all the deficiency diseases and not just scurvy.

It is possible that the skeletal lesions of scurvy occurring in late childhood and in adolescence may remain in young adults, including changes to the skull and to the long bones[13, 14]. In the human bones from the *Mary Rose*, there are lesions of the eye sockets (Plate 9) and evidence of blood clots along some long bones (Plate 10). These may be the result of adolescent scurvy. A number of skulls also have a pitting of the surface (Plate 11) which may be healed lesions resulting from the disease. We must be cautious, though, in our attempts at diagnosis, since various conditions can produce new bone along the long bone shafts. Such conditions include varicose veins, or localised accidents to bones that lie near the skin surface, such as the tibia. The diagnosis of lesions on the skull and in the orbits can also be controversial, since other forms of malnutrition can produce similar changes to those described above.

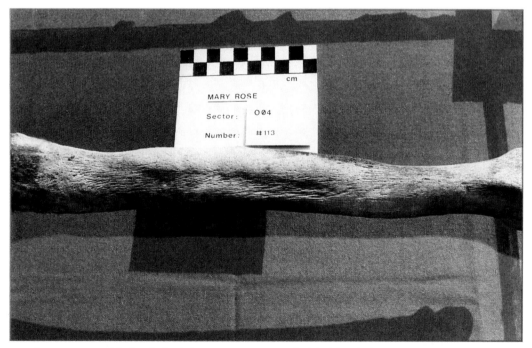

Plate 10. Possible healed adolescent scurvy. Probable blood clots along a tibia: FCS #14.

Plate 11. Healed porosity of
the skull: adolescent scurvy?

Another disorder produced by malnutrition is iron deficiency anaemia. Iron deficiency is the commonest world-wide cause of anaemia today[15] and it is also likely to have been common in the past. It is caused by an inadequate amount of iron in the diet, a loss of iron through persistent diarrhoea, or chronic blood loss through parasitic infection in the gut[16]. Some consider that certain lesions of the skull and orbits are associated with the disease[17] but this is not a generally held view[18]. Other metabolic or infectious diseases can also produce similar lesions[19].

Although it would be exciting to be able to differentiate between scurvy and iron deficiency anaemia in archaeological dry bone, there are difficulties associated with this. Rickets, scurvy or iron deficiency anaemia can occur in any combination with any or all of the other diseases of malnutrition, making differential diagnosis between the three conditions difficult in an individual skeleton. As Steinbock says:

"Malnutrition is almost always multiple"[20]

It is clear that there is evidence for malnutrition among the crew of the Mary Rose. Much of this will have been due to childhood disease, the effects of which remained in the skeletons of the young adults. As we have seen earlier (Chapter 3), famine was a persistent problem in the early sixteenth century, and some evidence for this persists in the bones of these men. A number of them had suffered from rickets and osteomalacia and probably from scurvy. The nature of their on-board diet (Chapter 4), as well as that when on land, meant that malnutrition may have been an additional problem for them as adults. Malnutrition, of course, will not have been the only problem that they endured during childhood.

Enamel hypoplasia is the name given to horizontal bands or to patterns of pits which form in the tooth enamel during childhood, and which may still be present in the adult teeth. When the condition is apparent in the adult teeth of archaeological skeletons, it has sometimes been seen as evidence for childhood dietary stress or deficiency. Hypoplastic defects are formed when the skeleton, including the teeth, stops growing. The dental enamel is no longer laid down when this happens and the bands or pits are left as markers on the teeth. Dietary stress is not, however, the only cause of interrupted growth in a child. Any systemic upset, such as the common viral diseases like measles and mumps, can cause a child to stop growing. All may leave the characteristic markers of enamel hypoplasia on a child's teeth. These defects can, therefore, be formed during childhood whenever growth stops for any length of time, whatever the cause may be.

The teeth of the crew of the *Mary Rose* do show evidence of some enamel hypoplasia. Seven per cent of the adult teeth had these defects. Most of the events that caused them seem to have happened between the ages of eighteen months and six years, based on measurement of the position of these defects on the adult teeth. Infants will have been weaned during these years. Weaning can produce its own dietary stresses, as well as any that may have been caused by the effects of famine. For instance, the majority of the crew, who were in their twenties, will have been born during the 1520's and will have been young children during the severe winter famine of 1527–28. In addition, the period from eighteen months to six years is one of frequent childhood illnesses, serious bouts of which will also have caused growth to stop and, probably, enamel hypoplasia to form on the teeth.

INFECTIOUS DISEASE

There is very little evidence for infectious disease in these skeletons from the *Mary Rose*. The common childhood viral infections such as measles and mumps are acute and do not last long enough to affect bone although, as we have seen, they can leave hypoplastic bands on the teeth. Other infections, however, are chronic and long lasting and may affect the skeleton. These include such diseases as syphilis[21], leprosy and tuberculosis. Although there is no evidence for either syphilis or leprosy in the crew, there is some evidence for a respiratory disease which may have been tuberculosis.

Microscopic techniques, including Scanning Electron Microscopy (SEM), have been used to examine lesions that are often found on the inner

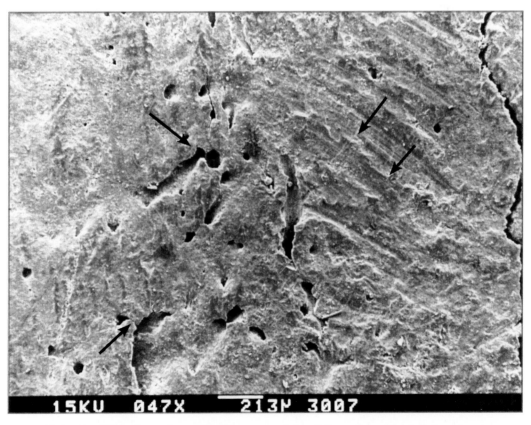

Plate 12. SEM of new bone forming on a visceral rib surface. The left-hand arrows indicate a new channel with an incipient roof and the right-hand arrows indicate areas of sand abrasion.

Plate 13. SEM of a new, completely roofed channel in the same rib (left-hand arrow) and an area of new bone formation (right-hand arrow).

(visceral) surfaces of the ribs, where this surface is in contact with the pleural membrane covering the lung[22]. The lesions are in the form of new bone laid down in the periosteum and, therefore, on top of the original cortical bone surface of the rib. There are many vascular channels in this new bone, which eventually become roofed-over, creating the new, external bone surface[22]. The fact that the visceral rib surfaces are affected, where they are close to the lungs, and the relatively large number of these changes in skeletal collections in both the Old and the New Worlds, suggests that they are associated with a fairly common respiratory disease. In the New World collections, where the rib lesions occur and the cause of death is known, they have been related to chronic pulmonary tuberculosis[22]. There are similar lesions on two adult ribs from the Mary Rose. Although the bone surface has been largely abraded by the action of sand and sea, SEM pictures clearly show areas of new bone formation, such as that illustrated in Plate 12. New vascular channels are forming with incipient 'roofs' (Plate 13) which in other areas become a complete bar of bone. These new channels can be clearly distinguished from the normal bone surface away from the lesion area, where there are many straight scratch marks probably caused by sand abrasion. Although the channels are small, their microscopic appearance is similar to those on the ribs from other skeletal collections[22, 23]. So, it seems possible that one or two members of the ship's crew had a chronic lung infection that may have been tuberculosis.

There are other pathological lesions in the group of bones from the ship, as well as those representing disease which were discussed above. These other lesions represent various conditions, some common and some unusual. We will discuss the common ones first.

FRACTURES

Although these bones represent the fighting men from a Tudor warship, there are relatively few fractures in the group. Those that are present occur in various bones of the skeleton. For example, there are three fractured ankles and one severely strained ankle. The fractures at the ankle are of the left fibula in every case, while the strain involves the supporting lateral ligaments of both a left tibia and fibula. An inward (adduction) force applied to the ankle, which is not severe enough to cause a complete rupture of these ligaments, produces a strain like this[24]. The fractures cause a shearing of the lower (distal) end of the fibula[25] when the ankle is pulled and twisted away from the body, for example in a bad fall or a jump onto an unstable surface. Another fracture, involving leg bones, is that of a right tibia and fibula. In this case, both bones have a spiral fracture which has not been re-set, see Plate 14. This kind of fracture is caused by a twisting force applied to the bone such as happens when an individual falls off a horse, leaving a foot behind in one stirrup, or tries to stride on over rough ground, leaving one boot stuck in the mud. Perhaps falling off a spar or beam on a ship, leaving a leg behind in the ropes or rigging would have a similar effect. When a fracture like this affects both bones, it usually happens at different levels in each bone[26]. In the present case, the distal tibia and the upper (proximal) fibula are affected (Plate 14). The fracture has not been

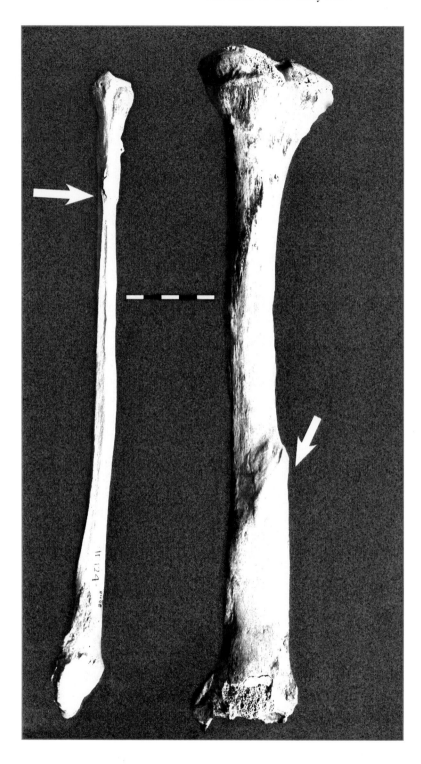

Plate 14.
Untreated, healed
spiral fracture of
a right tibia and
fibula. The fractures
have occurred at
a different level in
each bone (arrows).

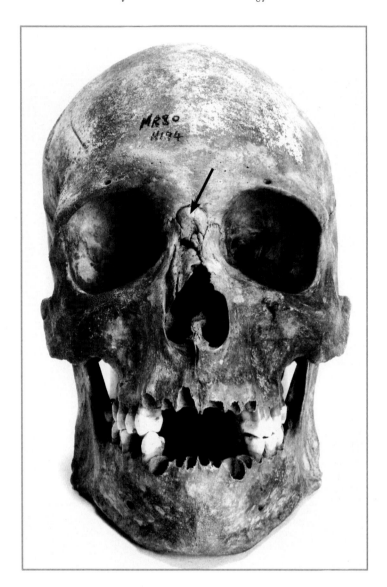

Plate 15. Healed fracture of the nasal bone (arrow).

re-set or the leg immobilised, so the affected bones have healed in their fractured positions, with a characteristic 'step' (Plate 14, arrows).

There are also fractures of other parts of the skeleton in this group. For example, there is an old fracture of a nasal bone, where the bone has clearly healed after the injury (Plate 15). There are also two other possible nasal fractures, although one of them is not as well healed as the others and may have occurred around the time of death. There are two healed fractures of the breastbone (sternum, figure 12). One of these affects an individual with a possible nasal fracture and an old, healed fracture at the chest (sternal) end of

Plate 16. Traumatised and arthritic right elbow.

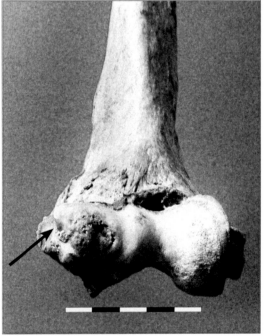

Plate 17. Traumatised and arthritic right elbow.

a rib. This man seems to have suffered some injury to his upper right abdomen, which resulted in these fractures. One other breastbone has an old, healed hole that perforates the bone. Since the breastbone is rather dense, considerable force must have been used to cause such a perforation.

There are, perhaps surprisingly, few rib fractures present in these bones for the crew of a warship. Including the one mentioned above, there are only seven surviving ribs with healed fractures, four of them probably belonging to one man. While it is possible that not many of the men had chest injuries, there is also another possible explanation. Perhaps the men were wearing some form of body protection, in the form of half-armour or padded jerkins. The remains of some breastplates were certainly found during the excavation[27] so they

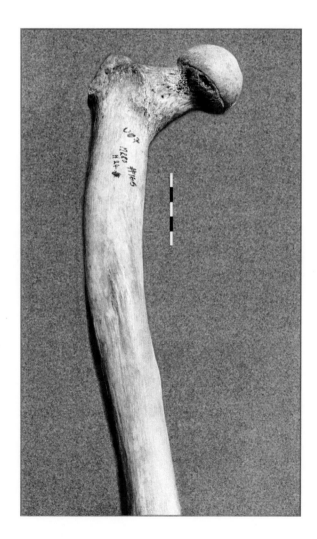

Plate 18. Old, bowing fracture of the right femur.

would have been available. While such protection would not save them from severe injury by arrow penetration[28], it might have helped to protect the rib cage from blows.

One heel (calcaneus), one ulna and part of a spine all have evidence of old, healed fractures. Two of the FCS skeletons have severely affected right elbow joints; both are from young adults. FCS#44 has a badly damaged right elbow, with destruction of the cartilage and a lower arm that, in life, could not have been straightened from the elbow. Osteoarthritis has already set in and the elbow looks as if it had been fractured, perhaps by a fall, when the epiphyses were fusing as the lad stopped growing. The second individual (#75), also has an arthritic right elbow, affecting all three bones with new bone growth (Plate 16) and matching patches of eburnation (bone-on-bone 'ivory' polishing, Plate 17). The reason for the damaged elbow is not clear in this case. There is one young adult right femur that has a healed fracture of the upper shaft. The bone is bent and twisted (Plate 18), the head of the femur is lower than it should be and there is matching damage in the right hip socket. This is probably an old childhood fracture, known as a 'bowing fracture'.

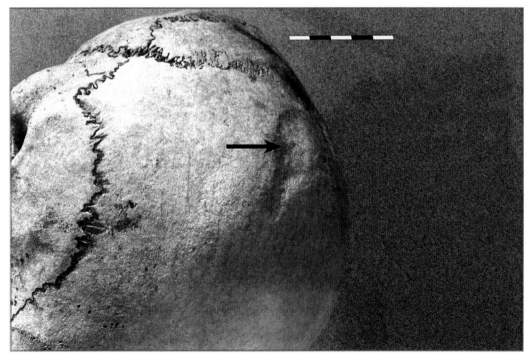

Plate 19. Probable depressed fracture of the skull (arrow).

Plate 20. Cranial wound caused by a penetrating missile. The wound was in the process of healing (arrow).

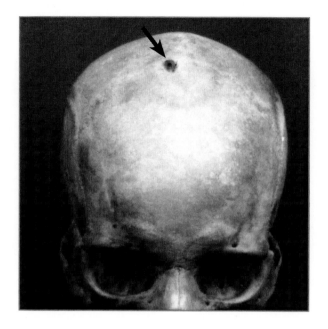

It would be tempting to say that most of the above fractures were caused by life on a Tudor warship but it is impossible to be sure that this is so. Some of them obviously occurred during childhood and others may have been the result of accidents away from the ship. However, there are fourteen cases of head injuries that are not all fractures and these may have belonged to fighting men on the ship. There are shallow depressions on the surface of some skulls which are probably the remnants of depressed fractures (Plate 19) but other, obviously penetrating wounds were clearly not fractures at all (Plate 20). A blunt instrument, such as a spar, probably caused the depressed fractures but a sharp missile, such as a bodkin arrowhead, would have caused the penetrating wounds, like that shown in Plate 20. The angle of penetration in the top of this skull suggests that the arrow was shot from above, and the man survived the attack, to drown later on the ship. He was probably wearing a helmet, and small fragments of helmets were found during the excavation of the wreck[27]. The bone around the wound was healing, however, so the attack was a fairly recent one. Alternatively, it has been suggested that a practice arrow at the butts, rather than during battle, could have caused this wound. In the former case, the bodkin arrowhead would have been wrapped, so that it did not cause permanent injury or death, although it may have penetrated his helmet. During battle, however, the arrow would have been naked and would easily have penetrated any helmet, probably fatally[28].

Avulsion Fractures

So far, we have discussed the type of fractures which are familiar to most people. These were usually untreated in the past, before methods of re-alignment and splinting were widespread, and so there is often evidence left for us to see on the skeleton. There are also other kinds of fractures which leave evidence on the skeleton, but which are perhaps not as familiar. These are avulsion fractures of various kinds, in which a piece of bone is traumatically torn away leaving an unhealed lesion on the bone. Fractures like these can occur where ligaments or tendons attach[29], and they are more common at some skeletal sites than others. For example, avulsion fractures can occur at the top of the tibia, just below the knee, at the inside edge of the elbow on the distal end of the humerus and at the fifth metatarsal on the outside edge of the top of the foot. Some of the *Mary Rose* men have avulsion fractures at these sites.

There are six examples of an avulsion fracture just below the knee, where a piece of the tibial tubercle has been pulled off by the action of the

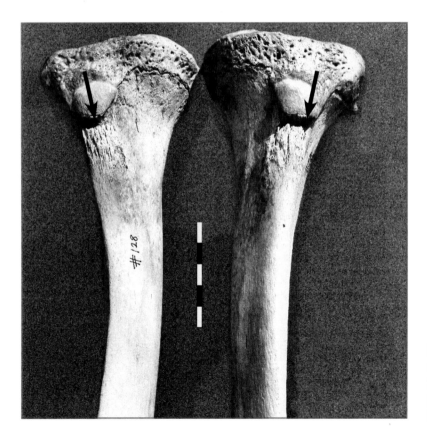

Plate 21. Avulsion of the tibial tubercle in a young adult (arrows).

tendon for the knee-cap (patella; see Plate 21). This tendon is a part of the quadriceps group of muscles which are involved in extension (horizontal straightening) of the knee. Rupture of the tendon is caused by a sudden flexion force applied to the lower part of the leg, which is resisted by the sharp contraction of the quadriceps muscles at the knee[30]. The combination of these two forces can cause the patella tendon to rupture on the tibia, sometimes taking a fragment of bone with it (Plate 21). Jumping on to an unstable surface, such as the moving deck of a ship, could cause the rupture. There are also avulsion fractures of the fifth metatarsal on the outer, upper edge of the foot (see figure 14). If there is a sudden, strong inward force on the foot, the tubercle at the base of this bone may be torn off by the action of the attached muscle and its tendon. There are three fifth metatarsals from the ship which have this condition (Plate 22). Plate 22 shows a foot where

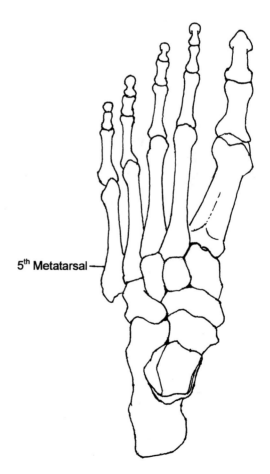

5th Metatarsal

Figure 14. The human foot.

Plate 22. Avulsion of the base of the fifth metatarsal. The piece of bone has been torn off by the attachment (arrows).

the injury had happened fairly recently, since the two pieces of bone are healing and would probably have united fully had the man not drowned. A bad jump or fall, when the foot is bent sharply inwards under the body, causes such injuries. A sixteenth century warship, such as the *Mary Rose*, will have been an unstable environment in which to live and work. Avulsion injuries like these of the knee and feet are not common in other medieval burial groups, which usually consist of parish or religious communities. Perhaps what we are seeing in this group are the remains of some of the mariners, where climbing, running and jumping in the environment of a fighting ship has caused these injuries.

Other Forms of Fractures
Other forms of fractures can affect the joint surfaces at the ends of some bones. Sometimes, usually as the result of an accident, the joint surface of a young, immature bone is damaged. When this happens, part of the blood supply

Plate 23. Transchondral fractures (osteochondritis dissecans) of the distal femoral condyles at the knee (arrows).

Plate 24. Posterior hip joint (acetabular) rim fracture (arrow).

is blocked and a piece of cartilage, or cartilage and bone, dies and falls off, leaving a characteristic hole or scar. This is fairly common in young boys and is particularly associated with damage to the knee in some sports, such as rugby football. It is known as transchondral fracturing and is caused by either shearing, side impact or rotation forces[31]. The most usual site for the injury is at the knee, on the end of the femur (Plate 23), but other sites may be involved as well[32].

A number of these fractures occur in the *Mary Rose* burials. There are 6 at the knee (Plate 23) 12 at the elbow and 11 on the big toe (first metatarsal, figure 14) of the foot. The elbow and the big toe are the most commonly affected sites in these men, which is interesting since these fractures are usually more common at the knee. Clearly, these men suffered greater stresses of the elbow and the big toe than they did of the knee. We must remember, however, that this sample represents only about 43 per cent of the crew and the frequency of these fractures in the whole crew is, therefore, unknown.

Fracture and Fracture-Dislocations of the Hip
A form of dislocation which affects the hip joint also involves the femur. There are three types of this injury:

1. Posterior (backward) dislocation or fracture-dislocation;
2. Anterior (forward) dislocation;
3. Central fracture-dislocation.

Posterior dislocation is the commonest form, where the head of the femur is forced out of the back of the hip joint. This happens when violence is applied to the shaft of the bone while the knee is bent. It is the kind of injury that occurs during a head-on car crash, for example, when the knee hits the internal bodywork of the car full on[33]. The head of the femur frequently carries a fragment of the posterior rim of the hip joint with it, causing the fracture-dislocation (Plate 24). The femur may or may not be seriously damaged.

There are five cases of fracture of the rim of the hip joint in the younger members of the *Mary Rose* crew. Both sides of the pelvis are affected in two individuals, the right side only in two and the left side only in one (Plate 24). All of these are posterior fracture-dislocations of the femur. There are also six examples of pits occurring in the top part of the femoral head

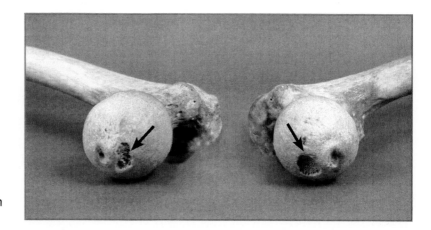

Plate 25. Pits in femoral heads, probably caused by a posterior fracture-dislocation (arrows).

both bilaterally, (Plate 25), and on one side only. These pits look similar to transchondral fractures and were originally diagnosed as such[34]. However, in two cases, FCS#9 and #39, there are also hip joint rim fractures. FCS#9 has the fracture on the left and FCS#39 on the right and there is a matching pit in the femoral head in both. Looking at these men, it does seem possible that posterior dislocations of the thigh can be accompanied sometimes by hip joint rim fractures and sometimes by pits in the head of the femur.

OSTEOARTHRITIS

Osteoarthritis is the most common disease to affect joint surfaces, both in modern populations and in archaeological groups[35]. It is often given other names of which the commonest is Degenerative Joint Disease. In the disease, there is a loss of cartilage at the joint surface, followed by a reaction of the exposed bone on this surface and at the joint margins[35]. Osteoarthritis only affects the synovial (freely moving) joints but, although these form the majority of the joints in the skeleton, it affects some of them more than others. These include the joints of the hands, the feet, the hip and the knee. Its frequency increases with age and, contrary to popular belief, its presence cannot necessarily be seen as a result of the practise of a particular activity or occupation.

Osteoarthritis is characterised by the presence of bone-on-bone polishing (eburnation) on a joint surface. Such polishing occurs when the cartilage has gone. New spurs of bone at the edges of joints (marginal osteophytes) may also occur, together with new bone or with pitting on the joint surface, the contours of which may be altered. In order to diagnose osteoarthritis in a skeleton, either eburnation or at least two of the other features should be present[35].

Osteoarthritis has been assessed separately for the spine and for the rest of the skeleton in the group from the *Mary Rose*. The spine will be discussed in Chapter 8 but osteoarthritis also occurs elsewhere in these men. For example, the pathological elbows discussed above (FCS#44 and #75) are both arthritic, with eburnation, pitting, new spurs of bone and altered joint contours (Plates 16 and 17). In addition, there are a further 63 examples of osteoarthritis in the group. Much of this osteoarthritis affected the articular surfaces of ribs and most of it occurred in men over 30, however, showing an increase with age.

Having considered the general pathology of the skeleton crew of the *Mary Rose*, what conclusions can we draw from the evidence? Firstly, let us look at the categories of general pathology. It is clear from the section on dietary deficiencies that these men had suffered from some malnutrition as children. Given their average ages, this is hardly surprising. Most of them will have been born in the 1520's, a time when famine was periodically widespread. In particular, the severe winter famine of 1527–28 will probably have affected some of them. From the few examples of osteomalacia, a small number of them appear to have suffered from dietary deficiencies as adults. As the bones are well-healed, however, these deficiencies probably occurred before they joined the ship. It is also probable that they contracted the normal viral childhood diseases, such as measles and mumps, and may have had some lung infection as adults. The complete lack of evidence for other adult infections, such as leprosy or syphilis, implies that they were healthier than many of their contemporaries. For example, there are examples of both these diseases, as well as tuberculosis, in the roughly comparable cemetery from Magdalen Street, Norwich.

As far as the evidence for trauma or accident is concerned, there are few cases of fractures. Most of these involve the hips, legs and/or feet in one form or another. They may reflect life in the unstable and slippery environment of a Tudor warship. There are a few depressed fractures of the skull, and very few of ribs. In comparison, the men from the Norwich cemetery suffered severe fractures of skulls and arms in particular, and were obviously subjected to a fair amount of interpersonal violence. These men came from the poorest parish in medieval Norwich and had probably fought at the battles of Crécy and Agincourt, as part of retinues. There is little osteoarthritis in the ship's crew, apart from that related to age.

In summary, the crew was generally robust and healthy and probably fairly well fed, at least by comparison with their contemporaries. Their bones are large and strong with little general pathology, apart from some related to childhood illness and some probably related to ship-board life. These are general statements, however, and do not relate to any effects that the practise of particular occupations or activities may have had on these men. These effects will be considered in the next chapter.

NOTES

1. Sharman, in Watt *et al.*, p. 25.
2. Ortner and Putschar, p. 278.
3. *Op. cit.*, p. 280.
4. Roberts and Manchester, p. 171.
5. Watt, in Watt *et al.*, pp. 58–9.
6. Taylor, in Watt *et al.*, p. 36.
7. Sharman *op. cit.*, p. 17. The slang term 'limey', used by Americans to identify the English, arose from the habit of referring to British ships and sailors in the West Indies during the nineteenth century as 'lime-juicers' or 'limeys'. Because of the widespread growth of limes in the West Indies, the lemon juice ration was often referred to as lime juice, hence the above terms. Sharman *op. cit.*, p. 24.
8. Steinbock, p. 254.
9. Ortner *et al.*, 1999.
10. Ortner and Eriksen, 1997.
11. Maat, p. 83.
12. Steinbock, pp. 256–8.
13. Mensforth *et al.*, p. 45.
14. D. J. Ortner, personal communication, 2000.
15. Steinbock, p. 230.
16. *Op. cit.*, p. 231.
17. Roberts and Manchester, p. 167.
18. Tony Waldron, personal communication, 2000.
19. Ortner and Putschar, p. 258.
20. Steinbock, p. 232.
21. Syphilis is one form of Treponematosis. There are four forms of this disease in all: Pinta, which only affects the skin; endemic syphilis (Bejel); Yaws; congenital (caught from an infected mother before birth) and acquired syphilis, both the venereal form. Bejel, yaws and venereal syphilis can all affect the skeleton.

22. Wakely *et al.*, 1991.
23. J. Wakely, personal communication, 2000.
24. Adams, 1982, p. 271 and figure 266, number 7.
25. *Op. cit.*, figure 266, number 1.
26. *Op. cit.*, p. 248.
27. Alexzandra Hildred, personal communication, 2000.
28. Simon Stanley, personal communication, 2000.
29. A ligament attaches one bone to another; for example, the small bones of the hands and feet are held together by ligaments. A tendon, on the other hand, attaches a muscle to bone.
30. Adams, 1981, p. 394 and figure 302.
31. Resnick and Niwayama, 1981, pp. 2257–8.
32. *Op cit.*, pps 2261–72.
33. Adams, 1982, pp. 194–5.
34. I. Watt, personal communication, 1986.
35. Rogers and Waldron, 1995, pp. 32, 44.

EIGHT

Occupation and Activity

T
he main objective of the analysis of a group of archaeological
skeletons is to present a clear picture of the living individuals
represented by their dry bones. The bones are the closest we will
get to the people themselves and we hope that they may hold the answers
to many questions about these people and their day-to-day lives. Because
the human skeletal collection from the *Mary Rose* represents about 43 per
cent of the crew of a Tudor warship, it is a unique collection. We know
that the complement of the ship consisted of the crew of 200 mariners plus
a group of 185 soldiers and 30 gunners[1]. So far, we have seen that they
were predominantly a group of young men, with an average height of about
171cm (5' 7"). They were strong, fit and healthy and probably looked quite
like us. The bones showed that they had a variety of pathological lesions,
some associated with dietary deficiencies, which probably occurred during
childhood or adolescence. Others lesions seemed to be related to accidental
events that may have happened as a result of their life on board ship (see
Chapter 7). Can we gain more information from these bones?

We want to know as much as possible, of course, about the people we are
studying, including the kind of work they may have been doing. One way we
do this is by analysing some of the changes to their skeletons and relating these
changes to the real or suspected activities in which the people were involved[2].
Here lies the rub, however, since we often know so little about the people
excavated from an archaeological site and have no clear idea about what work
they did. One way of finding out is to compare the observed skeletal changes

with those that occur in sports injury in the living and this can be a useful source of information. In recent years, Repetitive Strain Injury (RSI) associated with an activity such as constant keyboard use has shown that work can also produce identifiable problems[3]. In order to try and understand the work and activity patterns of the dead from their skeletons, however, we must take into account the following:

1. The age of the individuals showing the particular changes.
This is most important, since some changes that occur in the skeleton do so as a result of normal ageing processes[4].

2. The method by which muscles function.
Muscles do not work on their own but together in groups. For example, when we lift an arm, a whole group of muscles attaching to the shoulder and upper arm is involved in the action. We cannot, therefore, analyse the attachment of one single muscle on an arm bone and guess, from its development, what that person was doing.

3. The basic asymmetry which is present in the human skeleton.
Contrary to appearances in the living, we are not completely bilaterally symmetrical. So, the development of one arm in preference to the other, for example, should not necessarily be attributed to activity or occupation. There is an underlying congenital asymmetry which affects the arms.

These three factors must be taken into account when trying to decide exactly what people were doing by observing their skeletal changes[5]. This is particularly the case for most archaeological groups of skeletons, where we have no idea of actual occupations. In the case of the men from the Mary Rose, of course, we do have some idea of their activities, but it was essential to consider the above three factors when deciding whether it was possible to determine any of their occupations from their skeletons.

THE ARCHERS

There was surprisingly little damage to the wooden structure of the wreck of the *Mary Rose*, considering that she had been buried in seabed silts for 437 years. In an attempt to explain this, experimental work was done to try to

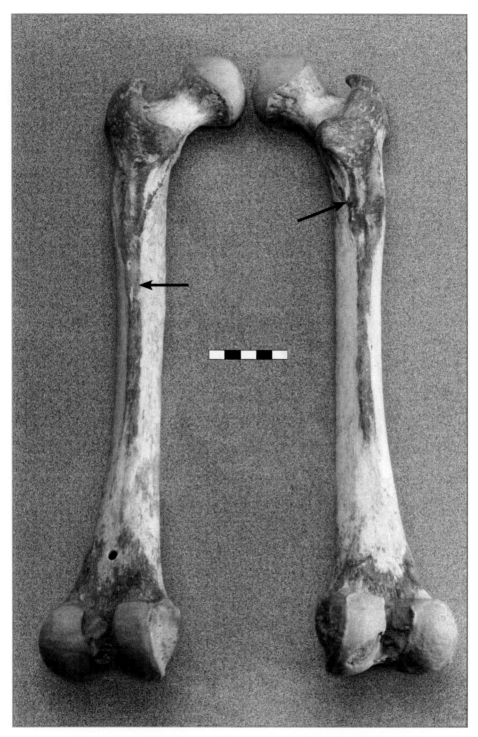

Plate 26. A pair of beautifully preserved femurs with clear and prominent muscle attachments (arrows).

decide how quickly the ship silted up after she was wrecked, and whether this had made any difference to her condition. Different kinds of wood were buried at different depths on the seabed and periodically examined for damage and decay. The results suggested that the wreck filled quickly with fine silts, probably in a few months after her sinking. This conclusion was reached because of the excellent condition of the experimental wood that had been buried in a similar manner[6]. The human skeletal remains from the Mary Rose are also wonderfully well preserved because of their relatively rapid burial in similar anaerobic seabed silts[7]. The bones are also physically hard, with none of the friability that we often find in archaeological burials from land sites. They are much better preserved, for example, than some of the burials from the Norwich site. Many of the bones are complete and undamaged and there are unusually clear surface markings on them where tendons and ligaments were attached in life (Plate 26). All of this led me to think about the possibility of deciding whether individual bones had belonged to mariners or to soldiers, but it soon became obvious that it would not be possible to make these decisions with such a mixed group of bones, and I gave up the idea. As the examination and recording of these bones continued, however, it became apparent that there was a rather high frequency of a particular anomaly, which is usually quite rare, and this was puzzling. The anomaly involves a part of the shoulder blade (scapula), at the outside edge of the bar of bone known as the acromion (figure 15) where there is an epiphysis (see Appendix I). This epiphysis normally unites with the main part of the acromion by 18–19 years of age, but in approximately three per cent of individuals in modern populations this union does not happen[8]. The anomaly is called Os acromiale.

There are 207 shoulder blades from the ship (see Chapter 6). Twenty-six of these have os acromiale (12.5 per cent). Many of the shoulder blades are single, however, without their matching bone, so that it is impossible to say whether, in life, the os acromiale had affected both bones of a pair or just the one side. So, in order to evaluate the true frequency of os acromiale in this group of men I decided to assess only complete pairs of shoulder blades. There were 52 complete pairs of bones. Ten pairs of these have os acromiale: six pairs bilaterally (on both sides, Plate 27), three on the left side only and one on the right side only. This gives a frequency of 19 per cent and, since the incident in modern populations is usually from about three to six per cent, the frequency for these men is obviously much higher. If we take the 10 pairs of bones with

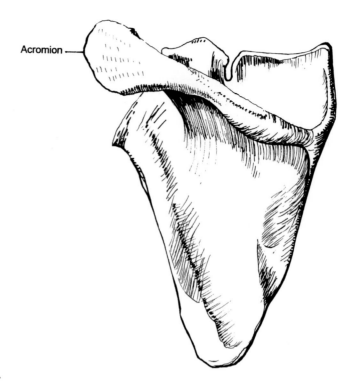

Acromion

Figure 15. The human scapula.

os acromiale, there are slightly more left shoulder blades (9) than right shoulder blades (7) with the condition. On the other hand, if we look at the 26 shoulder blades with the condition from the whole group of skeletons, 14.7 per cent (15 bones) have the defect on the left while 10.5 per cent (11 bones) have it on the right. So, whichever way we look at it, there is a slightly increased frequency of os acromiale on the left side in this group of men. All the affected bones belong to fully adult men, so this high frequency cannot simply be caused by skeletal immaturity. Can it be explained in any other way?

Os acromiale has often been considered as an anomaly that develops as the skeleton grows and matures, with the particular epiphysis failing to unite to the main bone. Others have suggested that it might be caused by a traumatic accident[9] and that it is more common bilaterally[10]. The latter is obviously the case in the *Mary Rose* group, where six of the ten pairs of shoulder blades have os acromiale on both sides. As the frequency is much higher with these men than in modern populations, I thought at first that some kind of traumatic accident might be responsible for this increase. It is, of course, difficult to visualise a trauma that would affect so many men in the same way, and this led me to speculate once again about a possible occupation or specialised pattern of activity that might have a similar effect.

During the medieval period every male was required to use a longbow from an early age and to practice with it[11]. This was based on a fourteenth century law that Henry VIII enforced soon after his accession, being a keen archer himself and always seeking to encourage the longbow and its use. The law stated that all fit males under the age of 60, excluding Judges and the Clergy and all who were "lame, decrepit or maimed", were to practise in the use of the longbow. Every boy aged from 7 to 17 had to be provided with a bow and two arrows by his father and, after 17, had to provide a bow and four arrows for himself[12]. Practice butts were also supplied in every town. In 1542 every man aged 24 and more was required to shoot to a mark 220 yards away (200m) to be acceptable for military service[12]. Of course, it is not clear how far this statute

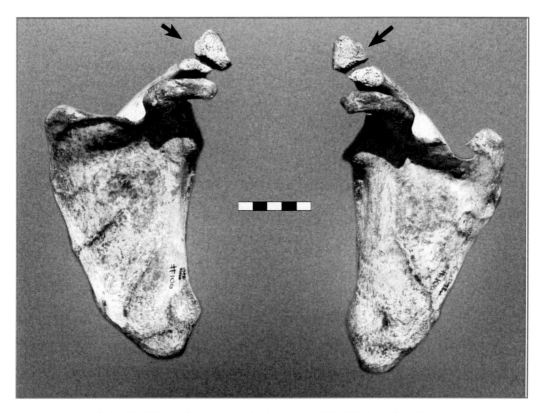

Plate 27. Bilateral os acromiale (arrows). FCS #7, found in the hold.
He may have been a war bow man.

was followed or enforced, particularly among the rural poor. The large number of longbows, arrows and other equipment recovered from the ship, however, does suggest that there were a considerable number of archers on board, even though they are not specifically mentioned in the Anthony Roll.

The Anthony Roll lists 250 yew longbows, 400 sheaves of livery arrows and six gross of bowstrings (864) in the inventory for the *Mary Rose*[13]. In fact, the remains of 172 long bows, 3,969 arrows, up to 18 leather spacers, pierced to take either 24 or 36 arrows, and armguards (bracers), mostly of leather and nearly all stamped with various marks were recovered from the ship[14]. Arrows were found either tied in bundles or in spacers of 24 arrows, so the 400 sheaves could have held a total of 9,600 arrows (400 × 24), or more if they held 36 arrows. Longbows marked with various stamps were also found and these, together with the livery arrows, suggest that there could have been a personal retinue on board (see Chapter 5). If so, we do not know whose retinue this was, particularly as there is no record of retinues at this late date. Alternatively, the stamps on the bows could be the bowyer's mark. War bows had to be made to a particular standard for maximum efficiency, so the makers of both good and of poor bows needed to be identifiable[15]. Of the 185 soldiers listed on the ship, some will probably have been longbow men. Interestingly, every ship in the Anthony Roll is listed as having longbows, which would seem to suggest that many mariners must also have used the bow[14]. So, there were probably many men on board who were capable of shooting the bow to the required distance for military service. This bow will have been a war bow.

The medieval longbow, particularly the war bow, was a very different weapon from that shot by archers today. A modern target archer shoots a short composite bow of about 20kg (45lb) draw weight but a medieval archer shot a longbow made from a single piece of wood (known as a self-bow) with a much heavier draw weight (see below). The draw weight is not the physical weight of the bow but the force required to pull back (draw) the bowstring in order to release the arrow. The draw length of the arrow controls the range of the bow[15], and there is a direct relationship between the length of the arrow and the length of the bow[16]. The medieval longbow was made from a round or D-sectioned yew stave, usually between 168cm (66 inches) and 183cm (72 inches) long. It was thicker in the middle and tapered towards the ends, which had horn nocks (slots) in which the bowstring rested. The wooden arrows varied in length between 71 and 76cm (28 to 30 inches) long and had a nock at the back to fit the bowstring. They were also fletched at the back, usually with three goose feathers, and the arrowheads were made of steel (iron and carbon), which is much harder than iron alone[17].

The technique employed in shooting the longbow was different from that used by a modern target archer. The modern archer draws the arrow back to a point on the chin or face, under the leading (aiming) eye: this is a fixed reference point. The archer stands sideways with both feet at an angle of 90° to the target. By contrast, the longbow man drew to the ear or the breast, aiming instinctively and with no fixed reference point (Plate 28)[18]. Medieval illustrations also show a different stance, with the leading (front) foot pointing towards the target. Modern longbow men who shoot

Plate 28. A modern longbow man a) at full draw and b) after release of the arrow. He is shooting a 'standard arrow' from a replica war bow of 54.5kg (120lb) draw weight. Photograph by courtesy of H.M. Greenland.

a replica war bow, such as those found on the *Mary Rose*, adopt a similar stance. The longbows could be shot either at close range or to a distance[15]. Plates 28 and 29 show 'clout' (distance) shooting, featuring replica war bows: the distance achieved in Plate 29 was 216m (237yd)[19]. To give the maximum range, the arrow is shot from the bow at an angle of 45° from the horizontal. Simon Stanley, the archer in Plate 29, is shooting a replica

Plate 29. Simon Stanley at full draw. Note the position of the drawing arm and his leading foot. The bow is 'The Leopard', here held at 75kg (165lb) draw weight, in April, 1995. Photograph by courtesy of Roy King.

war bow at exactly that angle. These replica war bows have extremely heavy draw weights. For example, the bow used in Plate 29 has a draw weight of 75kg (165lb) and it is thought that medieval war bows were of a comparable weight[15]. How do the bows from the *Mary Rose* compare with this?

In order to calculate their draw weights, five bows from the wreck were tested at the Imperial College of Science and Technology, London[20]. The five bows were fitted with horn nocks at either end, strung, and gently exercised with frequent rests until they could be fully braced as if for shooting. The bows were then drawn quickly in a machine, by a system of ropes and pulleys, to estimate the loading required to draw them to 76cm (30 inches). This draw length was chosen since the arrows from the ship vary from 71–76cm (28–30 inches), and it was decided to test for the longer arrow[20]. Computer modelling of these war bows had predicted draw weights of from 45.5kg (100lb) to 78kg (172lb) at a 30 inch draw, but they were so degraded by their sea burial that they could not be drawn properly to test their weights. At the same time, modern replicas of the *Mary Rose* bows (called MRA – Mary Rose Approximations) made of Oregon yew were also tested and the experimental results obtained by using these replica war bows were very close to the predictions for the *Mary Rose* originals[20]. However, the growth rings in the yew of one of the actual bows from the ship were much closer together than those in the Oregon yew from the modern tree. This means that the older yew was much denser and therefore stronger than the modern yew since it had grown much more slowly. It is likely, therefore, to have produced an even higher draw weight than those predicted. The persistent drawing of these heavy war bows must have had a significant effect on the archer.

In order to draw a longbow, the archer uses the major muscles of his arms and his shoulders. The elbow of the drawing arm (usually the right) is fully flexed, with the fingers of the hand (the middle two or three) exerting a pull on the string which corresponds to the draw weight of the bow[21]. As Hardy says:

"The pull on the fingers of the drawing hand corresponds to the weight of the bow, the left hand holding the bow, and the left arm being fully extended, but not locked. The shoulder muscles and the muscles which join the shoulder blades to the trunk contract strongly, and the right elbow is fully flexed. The effect of the natural elasticity of the bow is to swing the bow arm across the chest so, to counteract this, the shoulder muscles have to develop a pull of about 300lb (136kg) force to draw a 60lb (27.2kg) bow, which is five times as great as the pull exerted on the arrow. The resulting force across each shoulder joint, for the draw of a 60-lb bow, is greater than three hundredweight (152.4kg)"[22].

The forces used to draw the much heavier war bows would be even greater than this, and we must remember that these men were expected to use the bows regularly, both in wartime and in peace. The shooting technique obviously put great strain on the muscles of the back and of both shoulders. This assumes an equal use of the shoulders, however, which was not necessarily the case.

We saw earlier that every able-bodied male between the ages of 7 and 60 had to be trained in the use of the bow. This meant that, although there was no standing army during the Tudor period, all adult men could use a longbow, although some will have been more competent in its use than others. These were not the bows of mythology, such as those shot by 'Robin Hood and his Merry Men', neither were they the light, romantic longbows of which the Victorians were so fond[15]. They were extremely heavy and their continuous use would certainly have put great stresses on the shoulder muscles. But, the bow itself was not drawn and shot in the same way as a modern bow. Hugh Latimer in 1549, for example, described how his father instructed him to shoot:

"He taught me how to draw, how to lay my body in my bow, and not to draw with strength of arms as other nations do, but with strength of the body. I had my bows bought me according to my age and strength; as I increased in them, so my bows were made bigger and bigger, for men never shoot well, except they be brought up in it."[23]

W. Gilpin in 1791 stated that:

"the Englishman did not keep his left hand steady, and draw his bow with his right; but keeping his right at rest upon the nerve, he pressed the whole weight of his body into the horns of his bow. Hence probably arose the phrase "bending the bow", and the French of "drawing" one"[24].

This laying of the body into the bow, or leaning into the bow using the strength and weight of the body, would put a greater stress on the muscles of the left shoulder than on those of the right. This would certainly be the case for a right-handed archer, where the bow was held in the left hand (Plate 30 shows Simon Stanley laying his body into the bow). Given all the documentary and bone evidence, I reached two conclusions:

1. That the high frequency of os acromiale in the skeletons from the *Mary Rose* may be associated with the long-term use of the heavy war bow by some of the men.

Plate 30. Simon Stanley 'laying his body into' a 63.5kg (140lb) bow. By kind permission of H. D. Soar.

2. That the technique employed by the archers could account for the dominance of this condition on the left side[25].

If these conclusions are correct, however, why is there not a great deal more os acromiale present in groups of medieval male burials? After all, most of them will have been using the longbow for most of their lives, and many of them will have fought as archers at major battles both in the Wars of the Roses and abroad. Perhaps they were not all using heavy war bows? This idea led me to the further conclusion that the men with os acromiale may have been *specialist* archers, with the non-union of the acromion caused by the long-term stresses of using a particularly heavy war bow, probably from early adolescence.

Specialisation implies that some men were extremely skilful with the bow and were perhaps 'natural' archers who had diligently practised over many years. By the mid sixteenth century, however, the longbow was beginning to fade as the predominant weapon and there were fewer archers[15]. So, by this time, it is likely that only those men interested in, and good at, shooting the bow will have been the ones to spend longer than the required time in doing so. These more proficient men can probably be considered as specialists, although there is no documentary evidence for this. It is possible that such men will have been in demand, particularly on a ship like the *Mary Rose*. There are other bony changes in these men which may be related to the use of the heavy war bow and which almost certainly have a bearing on the high frequencies of os acromiale in the group.

During the 1990's I completed a research project which studied pairs of male humerus and femur bones from the *Mary Rose* and from the medieval parish cemetery in Norwich[26]. During the course of the research I attempted to answer the following question:

Were there any differences in length or other dimensions, which could be due to patterns of activity or occupation, between the pairs of bones from the two sites?

The research was based on a whole series of both standard and new measurements, particularly of the head of the humerus at the shoulder[27]. One new measurement was that of the area where the muscles involved in rotating and drawing the arm away from the body (abduction) attach to the head of the bone[27]. When these measurements were analysed, the left shoulder dimensions of the men from the *Mary Rose* were found to be larger than those of the men from Norwich. I speculated that this discrepancy in size was probably due to the presence of specialist archers in the *Mary Rose* group, especially given the high frequency of os acromiale. There will also have been archers present in the Norwich sample, since this cemetery was in use throughout the period covering the Battles of Crécy (AD 1346) and Agincourt (AD 1415) and the 100 Years War. English longbow men were certainly predominant in the first two conflicts and we know that men who could use the bow would be conscripted into retinues to serve in these wars. If they survived to return home, they would eventually be buried in their parish cemetery. Not surprisingly, then, os acromiale was also present in the Norwich men, but the frequency was not high (six per cent) and it occurred mainly on the right side. This suggests there were probably no specialist war bow men in the Norwich group.

A study of modern 'elite' Olympic archers showed that:

"During the course of an international event, a male archer will pull a bow 75 times a day for four days. This equals approximately 3,400lb (1545kg) pulled in a single day and represents an enormous strain on the bony, ligamentous and muscular structures of the shoulder girdle"[28].

The authors of this modern study found evidence for increased shoulder dimensions of the arm that holds the bow[28]. This is the left arm in most archers. It is, therefore, a reasonable assumption that what applies to a modern archer who pulls a relatively light, composite bow, will be even more applicable to a medieval archer pulling a heavy warbow. This does not mean that an individual male skeleton from a medieval cemetery may be identified as a professional archer, just because he has os acromiale on the left side. However, when measurements of two such groups of males are compared, increased dimensions of the left shoulder in one group, together with high frequencies of os acromiale, may well indicate the presence of specialist war bow men in that group. The crew of the Mary Rose seems to include such a group of specialists.

OTHER BONY CHANGES

Muscles are attached to bone by tendons, the sites of which often degenerate with age. This degeneration is usually in the form of ridges or spurs of new

Plate 31. New ridges and spurs of bone (known as enthesophytes) on the
distal fibula of a young adult (arrows).

bone[29], which are visible on the skeleton and can occur wherever tendons
attach (Plate 31). Although such ridges and spurs often occur as we get
older, they can also form at any age due, for example, to the chronic stresses
caused by the wear and tear of continual patterns of activity[30]. If we wish
to relate this kind of degeneration to patterns of activity, we must be sure
to draw our conclusions only from the study of young individuals. As far as
the *Mary Rose* crew is concerned, ridges and spurs of new bone were only
analysed for the FCS numbers. These were the only skeletons on the ship
which were complete enough to age with any accuracy and I needed to be
able to look at just the younger men.

Thirty-nine men (42 per cent) had the spurs and ridges of new bone
in the FCS group and twenty-three of them (25 per cent) were young. The
most frequently affected bone was the humerus and fifteen of the twenty-
three young men had changes to this bone. All the changes were on the upper
part of the humerus, affecting the area at which major muscles attach. These
muscles are involved in rotation and in movement of the arm towards or
across the chest (adduction, Plate 32). One quarter of the youngest of the
FCS skeletons had developed these changes which mostly affected the upper
arms and, considering their age, it is probable that that they were the result of
activity.

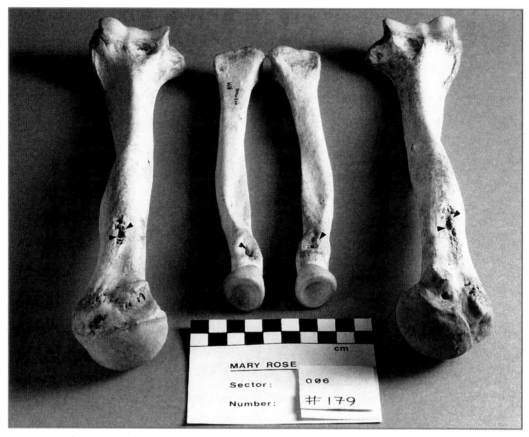

Plate 32. Enthesophytes on paired arm bones from a young adult (arrows).

Another form of bony proliferation occurring in this group affects the collarbone (clavicle) where the ligament that attaches the inner part of the bone to the first rib is affected (the costoclavicular ligament)[31]. This ligament acts, together with other muscles and ligaments, to help elevate the humerus at the shoulder and to stabilise the shoulder blade[32]. In a number of clavicles from the crew, there is a considerable build-up of bone where the ligament attaches. This has produced ridges of bone and, in some cases, deep impressions for the ligament (Plate 33). There are 16 examples of these changes in the youngest of the FCS group of skeletons although, as with the shoulder blades discussed earlier, some of them are only single bones and have not been included. Of the pairs of clavicles, seven have the changes in both bones and two have it on the right side only. We do not usually see this kind of bony reaction in younger people and, in the case of the crew, it is probably

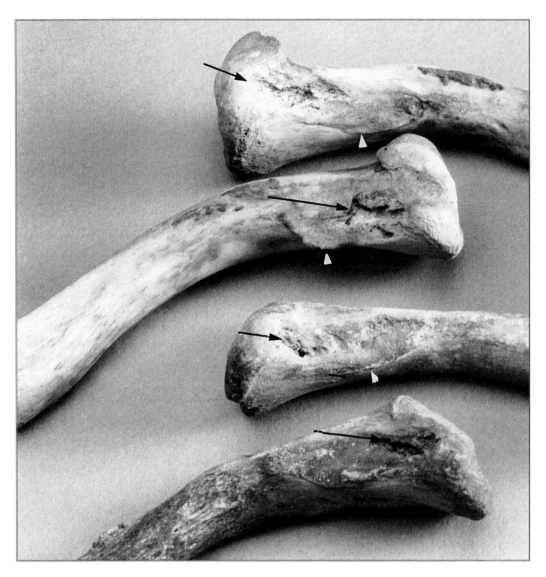

Plate 33. Enthesophytes in the form of ridges (arrowheads), and deep impressions for the costoclavicular ligaments (arrows).

associated with movements of the shoulder blade in raising and lowering of the arm. This raises questions as to why this particular bony reaction should be present in this group. It is a question to which I will return later. So far, we have considered only changes to the arms and shoulders of these men. There are other changes, particularly to the pelvis and the legs, which we should also consider.

133

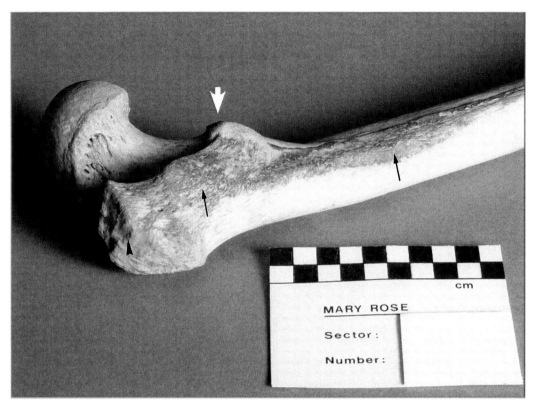

Plate 34. Proximal half of a femur from the Mary Rose, showing areas of major muscle attachment (arrows and arrowhead: greater trochanter).

In order to try and answer the recurring question about the relationship between bone dimensions and activity (see page 118), new measurements were created for the femur as well as for the humerus. These new measurements included some on the upper part of the femur where the major muscles attach (Plate 34). The amount of development of some muscle attachment areas was scored as well (Plate 34). This scoring was on a 0 – 4 basis, where 0 = no development at all and 4 = a very well developed area. For example, the femur illustrated in Plate 34 would score 2 on this scale. The *Mary Rose* men were compared with the men from Norwich see if there were differences in the legs as well as in the arms and shoulders.

The three gluteal muscles attach at the top of the femur, two of them on the large area of bone known as the greater trochanter (Plate 34). The greater trochanter is bigger on both sides in the men from the *Mary Rose* than it is in the Norwich men, leading to the idea that the crew members were involved in more activity using the gluteal muscles than were the other men. Two of these muscles work together to keep the pelvis stable and stop it tilting sideways. They would have to work hard on a ship like the *Mary Rose*, which had a small keel and very little ballast, and where the crew would often be trying to keep their balance. The third gluteal muscle is the largest in the buttock and, using the above scoring system, its attachment is more developed in the crew members, particularly on the right side, than in the Norwich men. This muscle is gluteus maximus and it is used in climbing and in balancing. It is also used to keep the trunk steady during various activities, including throwing and shooting a longbow.

The men from the *Mary Rose* had more developed thigh and buttock muscles than the men from Norwich, as we have just seen. There were also differences between them in the development of various muscles that attach to the pelvis and these are discussed in Appendix III[33]. In summary, the development of the pelvic muscles, as well as those on the thigh and buttock, all support the idea of a group of young men within the crew who were using heavy war bows.

THE 'GUN CREW'

One area of the skeleton that we have not yet discussed is the spine. The spine (vertebral column) is divided into three sections: the neck (cervical spine), the chest (thoracic spine) and the lower back (lumbar spine). Some of the spines from the *Mary Rose* group have enlarged and developed areas, particularly in the lower segments, and this is noticeable in such a young group of men.

A colleague and I recently made a number of interesting comparisons between the spines of the ship's crew and those of the men from the Norwich site[34]. The study involved a consideration of the four common types of pathological change that occur in the spine. These are:

1. Pitting (osteoarthritis) of the facet joints at the back (Plate 35);
2. Extra, new bone around joint surfaces (marginal osteophytes, Plate 36);
3. Pits in the vertebral body surfaces (Schmorl's nodes, Plate 37);
4. Ossified spinal ligaments: the central spinal ligaments are changed to bone (Plate 38).

Plate 35. Osteoarthritis (pitting) of the facet joints at the back of the spine (arrows).

Plate 36. Marginal osteophytes (extra, new bone around joints). In this example, the osteophytes have fused together (arrow).

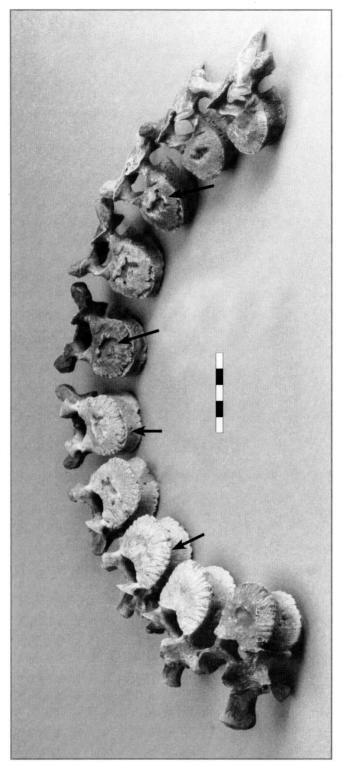

Plate 37. Schmorl's nodes (pits in vertebral body surfaces: arrows). This spine from the Mary Rose is from a young individual, exemplified by the unfused epiphyses and 'billowing' of the surfaces of the bones (arrowheads).

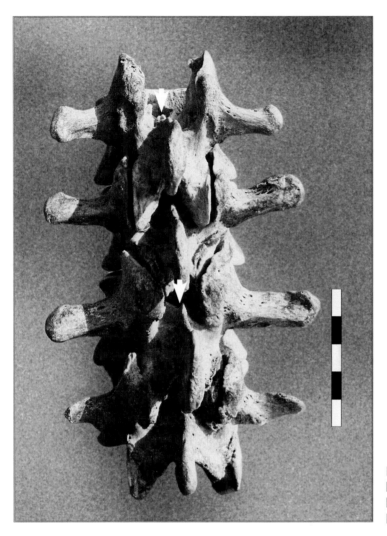

Plate 38. Ossified spinal ligaments (central spinal ligaments turned to bone, arrows).

Eighty-five per cent of the *Mary Rose* spines were from adolescents or young adults, while the Norwich spines were divided fairly equally, with fifty-four per cent coming from adolescents or young adults and forty-six per cent from mature and old adults. Very few of the spines from the ship's crew were affected by osteoarthritis, a result that didn't surprise us, since they were so young. More surprisingly, we found that the amount and distribution of the other three types of lesion between the two groups was quite similar[34], although there was more ossification of the spinal ligaments in the ship's crew. This ossification was so well developed in some cases that it was almost impossible to separate adjoining vertebrae (Plate 38). So, we found that the two groups of men were more alike in the amount and distribution of the common types of spinal pathology than we would have anticipated, given the differences in their ages. How could we explain this?

The majority of the men from the *Mary Rose* were adolescents or young adults, and this was evident from the fact that there were many unfused epiphyses (see Appendix I), including some from spines (Plate 37). Since the spinal changes between the two groups are so similar despite the age differences it seems that, in the *Mary Rose* men, spinal changes have been accelerated to produce lesions which are usually due to ageing. We concluded that this acceleration was probably related to the occupations of the crew. Many of the occupations aboard the ship would clearly have involved some heavy manual work and probably a great deal of heaving and hauling in fairly confined spaces. This would particularly apply to the gun crews. Is there evidence from any of the FCS skeletons that they could have been members of a gun crew?

There were two main types of large gun on board the *Mary Rose* when she sank. These were wrought iron breech-loading and bronze muzzle-loading guns[35]. The former were made by shrinking hoops of wrought iron on to an iron cylinder and they were mounted on a wooden sledge which was made from a hollowed tree, keyed for the gun. The sledge had one axle and two wheels at its centre. The gun was fired using a breechblock, which had to be lifted up and onto the top of the gun every time it was used. This block weighed 205.5kg (450lb) and would have needed four men to lift it[36]. The gun fired iron 'anti-ship' or stone 'anti-personnel' shot[35]. The large bronze muzzle-loading guns were cast, not wrought, and were a relatively new weapon[35]. They had elm carriages so that they could be run back from the gun port for cleaning and reloading. They fired iron shot and were used on the main gun deck. There were three large bronze guns on each side of this main deck, one in the bow, one amidships and one in the stern. Between the bronze guns there were four iron guns on each side[36]. As well as the big wrought iron and bronze guns, there were also hailshot pieces and iron breech-loading swivel guns, so the *Mary Rose* carried a lot of ordnance.

In terms of operating the guns on a warship, one of the more important factors for the men was the headroom (vertical space) on the main deck. Obviously, if exceedingly heavy breechblocks have to be lifted on and off the iron guns, and if the bronze guns have to be wheeled backwards and forward, this takes manpower. If there is not enough space between the main deck and the upper deck above, some of the men will not be able to work in an upright position. Looking at figure 7 (page 48), the conditions on the main deck seem to be rather cramped and it is difficult to imagine operating such big guns in this space. In reality, however, the headroom on this deck is 196cm forward (6' 5") and 183cm aft (6'), away from the main beams, which are nearly 305cm (10') apart[36]. Since the average height of the men was 171cm (5' 7") and the tallest was no more than 180cm (5' 11"), there should have been just enough vertical space for a gun crew to work without stooping on this deck. There may have been taller men in the rest of the crew who were not found, of course, and some of these may have been members of gun crews. Also, we are only talking about vertical working space. The length of some of these guns and the distance between them on the gun deck will have presented other problems.

Figure 16 shows where the FCS skeletons were found on the ship. Each of these skeletons was given an individual number as the bones were sorted and matched. When the sorting and matching was done, we found that some of these FCS skeletons were together in clusters or groups of men. This was generally in areas where there were a lot of men mixed up together and so we were able to sort them back into individuals. Several of these clusters from the main deck may be important in terms of the gun crews.

It is thought that a gun crew on the *Mary Rose* probably consisted of six men[36]. It is unlikely that any of the six would have been a longbow man. There would have been barely enough head room in which to draw and shoot a longbow, let alone cover the open gun port. This could only have been done from a kneeling position and it is impossible to draw a longbow while kneeling[15]. One of the six will have been the Master Gunner and these probably make up the thirty Gunners listed in the Anthony Roll. Six men would have been necessary to operate the heavy bronze guns by heaving and hauling them in and out of the gun ports. As far as the big wrought iron guns were concerned, four men would have been needed to lift the heavy breechblocks up and down. A Master Gunner was probably in charge of more than one gun, since the Mary Rose had a total of ninety-one guns altogether. This may have applied to his crew as well, but we have no idea how it worked in practice[36].

In sector 3 of the main deck (M3, see figure 10), a large bronze gun was found. This gun was a culverin with a 14cm (5½") internal bore, weighing 2.13 tonnes (2.1 tons) and 3.3m (11') long (Plate 39). In the same sector was a group of FCS skeletons, numbers 74–78 and 91 (figure 16), a total of six men. They were found in close association with the gun and, from the state

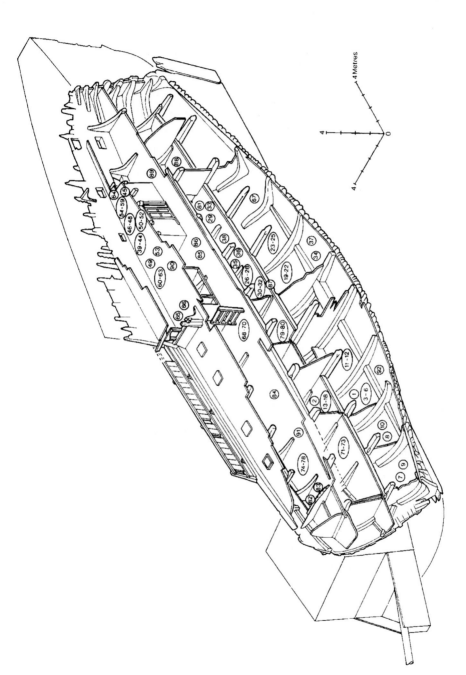

PORMR: SKELETAL MATERIAL LOCATIONS: FAIRLY COMPLETE SKELETONS

Figure 16. Isometric projection of the wreck, showing the distribution of the Fairly Complete Skeletons (FCS) by individual number. Copyright © the Mary Rose Trust.

of the bones, seemed to have lain in the same area for a long time. Could they have been part of a gun crew?

All six of these men were young, probably in their early to mid twenties. The shortest of them (#78) was about 160cm (5' 3") and the tallest (#91) was about 175cm (5' 9") in height. Apart from #78, all of them were strong, robust and with very well muscled skeletons. There is a marked amount of pathology in these men, particularly in some of the spines. Numbers 74, 75 and 77 have very stressed spines and, in the case of #74, the changes are extreme (Plates 36 and 38). There is new bone fusing two vertebrae together (Plate 36), and huge facet joints at the back with ossified spinal ligaments (see page 138 and Plate 38). The changes are so extreme that, in life, parts of this spine must have been locked together (Plate 38). Number 75 was one of the two men with an arthritic elbow (see Chapter 7, page 104). There are also changes to the spine, although not as extreme as those for #74. A lot of the skeleton is darkly stained, probably with iron, and there are crystals of iron oxide on many bones[37]. Although #77 has an incomplete spine, the surviving seven vertebrae and the sacrum all look as if they have been subjected to persistent, long term stresses. There is new bone where the sacrum and pelvis meet, on the facet joints at the back of the vertebrae, and on many of the muscle attachments on the pelvis. The whole of this man's lower back looks as if it had been subjected to strong pulling/pushing forces and resembles the spine of a much older man, although he was only in his early to mid twenties. Number 76 is another skeleton with darkly stained and encrusted bones. This man probably suffered from rickets as a child because the top halves of both his tibias are bowed (see Chapter 7, page 92). His spine shows some sign of stress, with pits in the surface of the vertebrae. All his bones are strong and with well-developed muscle attachments. Number 91 is described as "<u>very</u> strong and robust" on the skeleton recording sheet, with large bones. He is the tallest of the group and, like the others, has very well- developed muscle attachments. Like #76, he was only in his early twenties.

So far, we have discussed five men from this group in M3. The remaining skeleton is #78 and he is different from the others, although he is of a similar age to #76 and #91. He is the shortest of the group and, in comparison with the other skeletons, his bones are much more delicate, lacking the marked build-up of muscle attachments which we saw on the other five men. There is a small amount of stress of his spine, especially of the second neck vertebra, and some of the bones are darkly stained like others in the group. The difference in appearance of this skeleton, compared with the other five, is quite marked. He doesn't appear to 'fit' with the group but, since his bones are similarly stained, he seems to have been in the area of M3 for a long time and probably since the ship sank. Do we have the remnants of a gun crew here and, if so, can #78 possibly be part of that crew?

Plate 39. The large bronze culverin from M3, found with the skeletons of a number of men – the gun crew?

The work that was done on the spines of the Mary Rose crew showed us bones that should have belonged to much older men. This led us to believe that what we were seeing was probably a result of long-term stresses caused by various patterns of activity indulged in by the crew. The spine of #74 is extraordinary in its development, with huge joints and a lot of new bone (Plates 36 and 38). To a lesser extent, this also applies to #75 and #77. All the men in this group (apart from #78) have very well developed muscle attachments, especially given their youth. They were all found with one of the large bronze culverins (Plate 39) in an area where they seemed to have been trapped with or by the gun[36]. Many of the bones were stained brown and some had iron oxide crystals growing on them. They seemed to have been lying in the same area of the ship for a long time, probably since she had sunk. It is a reasonable assumption, therefore, that these men represent the remnants of a gun crew, although there is still the problem of #78. It is tempting to suggest that he might have been the equivalent of a powder monkey, used to carry the powder to the guns. He may, of course, have been nothing to do with the gun or its crew, but merely have been trapped in the area when the ship went down. His skeleton is certainly different from the others in the group and does not look as if he had been involved in very hard work.

In spite of the problems of trying to associate changes in skeletons to patterns of activity in the living people they represent, it seems possible to make some comments about the crew of the *Mary Rose*. We have seen that there is reasonable evidence from the bones for a specialist group of archers in the crew, although no archers are mentioned in the Anthony Roll. It is also likely that we have the remnants of a gun crew from part of the Main Deck of the ship. Since there are other spines with similar changes, there were probably other gun crew members elsewhere in the wreck. The archaeological evidence from the artefacts already discussed supports the skeletal evidence for such a group of men. For example, there is both archery and gunnery equipment from various areas of the ship and this is related to some of the skeletal remains.

We have discussed in detail the skeletal remains from the *Mary Rose* in the last three chapters. We now have to examine how the evidence from these remains relates to the historical and archaeological record and what further information, if any, they can give us.

NOTES

1. The crew is listed in the Anthony Roll – see Chapter 1, reference 7.
2. A fine example of this kind of work is the 1983 study by Merbs on a Canadian Inuit population.
3. Bird, 1990, pp. 49–52.
4. The presence of osteoarthritis increases in a population with age, as discussed in Chapter 7. The same also applies to the development of muscle attachment sites, which are known as enthesopathies. See Resnick and Niwayama, pp. 1297–1300.
5. For a full discussion of this entire topic see Stirland, 1992.
6. Alexzandra Hildred, personal communication, 2000.
7. An anaerobic environment is one in which there is no free oxygen present. In the case of the *Mary Rose*, this led to a slowing-down of the natural processes of decay, so that the preservation of many organic materials from the ship, including the human bone, is superb.
8. Stirland, 1984.
9. Miles, 1994.
10. See, for example, Nicholson *et al.*, 1996, Sterling *et al.*, 1995 and Liberson, 1937.
11. Trevelyan, 1947, p. 89.
12. Hardy, p. 218.
13. Livery arrows were part of the provision of equipment for retainers.
14. Alexzandra Hildred, personal communication, 2000.
15. Simon Stanley, personal communication, 2000.
16. Hardy, p. 9.
17. Rees, p. 24.
18. Bartlett and Embleton, p. 32.
19. H. D. Hewitt Soar, personal communication, 1999.
20. See Pratt in Hardy for a complete account of this work, pp. 212–13, 215–16.
21. One school of thought suggests that the English 'v' sign probably originated with the medieval warbow man. These archers were the most successful fighting infantry of the medieval period and caused great fear amongst their enemies, particularly the French. They could shoot their weapons with great accuracy and speed and the French threatened to cut off the two middle fingers of the shooting hand of any English archer they captured. So, in order to instil even more panic, the English archers developed the habit of waving those two fingers in the air at the French.
22. Hardy, pp. 150–1.
23. Hardy, p. 135.
24. Trevelyan, p. 18n.
25. Stirland, 1984.
26. Stirland, 1992.
27. Stirland, 1993, figures 3 and 4 and Table 1, p. 108.
28. Mann and Littke, pp. 85, 88.
29. Resnick and Niwayama, p. 1294.

30. Waldron, 1994, p. 101.
31. McMinn and Hutchings, pp. 93–4.
32. Gray, pp. 478–81.
33. Stirland 1992, pp. 200–2.
34. Stirland and Waldron, 1997, figs 4–6.
35. MRT 3, pp. 22–5.
36. Alexzandra Hildred, personal communication, 2000. See also fig. 6, p. 17, where these 7 guns are visible on the main deck of the port side of the ship.
37. The crystals largely consisted of red/brown haematite and blue vivianite. They had grown in cavities on some bones, such as hip joints (haematite), and under the cortical layer of others (vivianite). They were quite beautiful and unexpected and occurred on bones that had probably been in close proximity to iron in some form or another. They were also present on the two skeletons in M2: #82 and #83.

NINE

Conclusions

Ships, and their fate, have a special place in the British psyche – we feel a strong link with vessels both great and small. And so, when the *Mary Rose* was raised, on October the 11th 1982, and broke the surface of the sea, the whole country seemed to be watching. Many people knew that the *Mary Rose* had been the flagship of Henry VIII's Vice Admiral, Sir George Carew and that she had sunk with the loss of nearly all hands on July the 19th, 1545. They also knew that divers from all over the world, including HRH Prince Charles, had been working on her. What few people realised, however, was the amount and condition of the material that had been excavated from the ship, including the skeletal remains of her crew.

When the *Mary Rose* was placed in the cradle on the seabed (figure 4 c)) and then raised, she was still at an angle of 60° from the vertical. She remained at this angle while the cradle was placed on a barge and towed into Portsmouth harbour, to be housed in Number 3 Dry Dock. In 1984, however, it was decided to winch the hull upright and this work was completed in July 1985[1]. In August of that year, on one of my periodic visits to the Mary Rose Trust, I was taken on board the hull and stood in the hold, close to where the companionway had been (figure 7). This was a strange and rather frightening experience. The hull rose in front of me like a black, cold wall and everything was dripping as it was periodically misted with super-cooled fresh water. The lowest portholes capable of letting in natural light were the gun ports two decks above where I was standing and, for the first time, I realised how dark it would have been below decks in such ships. I was also made properly aware of the conditions under which the men had lived, worked and died, and it was this, together with the evidence from their bones, that provided the impetus for the research that led, eventually, to this book. Various questions arose during the course of this research which the book has attempted to answer and it would be useful to summarise them now.

The historical and documentary evidence gives us one set of 'facts', the archaeological evidence another. The first question is 'How do the two mesh together?' For example, why did the *Mary Rose* sink? From documentary evidence, the French claimed to have sunk her, but was there any archaeological evidence for this? When we look at the men, other questions occur. For example, how old were they and were they shorter than their modern counterparts, as has often been assumed? What was their diet and their general state of health? How were ships like the *Mary Rose* crewed? Documentary sources imply that men probably came from a wide area, but what does the archaeological and bone evidence tell us? From my point of view, the most important questions are those concerned with the men's occupations and life styles and whether it is possible to identify those from their skeletons. For example, is there any evidence for professional elements within the crew, and is it possible to identify any specific individuals? This chapter will draw together the evidence presented in the rest of the book and attempt to answer these questions.

There is no archaeological evidence that the French sank the *Mary Rose*, although their galleys were certainly in the process of engaging the English fleet and were capable of inflicting considerable damage on the large war ships. No damage was found in the hull to suggest she had been sunk by cannon fire. Rather, it is likely that the ship, being old and heavy, executed a clumsy manoeuvre in trying to present her broadside to the enemy. She then heeled, quickly took in water and sank. The majority of the men on board stood no chance of escape, even if they could swim, since they were trapped by the anti-boarding netting, which was stretched over all the exposed decks.

At the present time, archaeological evidence for the men's diet comprises meat and fish bones and some fruits. Further evidence may come to light as work continues on the preserved organic remains from the ship. The meat consists of beef and pork and one fallow deer haunch, probably for the officers. The beef had been butchered according to King's Regulations and consisted entirely of flat bones, devoid of marrow. It was all of a high quality from immature animals. There was one cask of pork, which included some marrow-containing long bones, as well as vertebrae and ribs. A large deposit of pork and ham, which had been butchered in quarters, was also found loose in the hull[2]. All the meat had been salted. The fish was stockfish and largely consisted of headless cod[2]. These victuals accord well with the documentary evidence. As well as plum stones and grape pips, there were the remains of grape skins in a barrel, although these could have been left from wine. There were broom pods; there was threshed rye straw for bedding and packaging, and hemp pollen from the large amount of rope which was on the ship[3]. Evidence for other victuals, for example bread, biscuit, beer, butter and cheese did not survive.

Although it is often assumed that the King's ships were crewed by men from the British Isles, particularly from England, the documentary evidence suggests otherwise. Difficulties in finding sufficient men in 1544–5 led to the impressment and/or enlistment of other nationals. It seemed unlikely that there would be any evidence of this from the skeletal remains. Some new work, however, has shown otherwise. This work has analysed the proportions of oxygen isotopes in some of the men's teeth. Water is composed of oxygen and hydrogen, the oxygen occurring as a mixture of isotopes, each of which has its own detectable signal. The oxygen isotope ratios in drinking water change from the equator to the pole, and vary according to latitude[4]. Since the signals are analysed from the teeth, which are formed during childhood, they provide information on where adults were living when they were children – in other words, where they originated. Tests showed that about twenty-five per cent of a small random sample of the men's teeth was found to originate from much further south than Britain[4]. The implication of these results was difficult to accept at first, since it had not occurred to me to doubt that Englishmen, mainly from the West Country, had crewed the King's ships. But further reading uncovered references to Italians, Spaniards and Greeks being pressed into Henry's service. Moreover, some beautiful Italian gun shields and hand guns were excavated from O10 on the orlop deck[5]. So, it seems that, as well as having the "Fleming among the survivors", the *Mary Rose* was also crewed from other, more southerly countries.

Some of the skeletal evidence suggests that there was a specialist group of warbow men among the crew. The medieval longbow has often had rather romantic connotations, but there was nothing romantic about the war bows, including those from the ship. Of immense draw weight, they would have required the application of great strength in the shoulders, arms and upper spine in order to draw and shoot them effectively. That the war bow was used with dramatic effect by the British is beyond doubt. The success of the English at the battles of Crécy and Agincourt is a matter of record, as is the well-founded French fear of the English bow men. The warhead on the arrows shot by the bows was a fearsome implement of destruction.

The archer in Plates 29 and 30, Simon Stanley, shoots a heavy replica war bow. He is also a traditional arrowsmith, making replica arrows and arrowheads. These arrowheads are made of steel in the style of the traditional bodkin (Plate 40). They weigh at least 40gm and are considerably heavier than their modern counterparts[6]. Bodkin arrowheads such as these were used from the 1380's until the longbow fell out of use as a weapon. If the bows from the *Mary Rose* were all between 61kg–75kg (135lb–160lb) draw weight, then the arrows needed to be 100gm–120gm to absorb all the energy of these very heavy bows and attain their target with full effect[6]. A falling arrow of this weight still has nearly as much energy as when it left the bow and can travel for at least 227m (250yd). Made of ash, birch or poplar, such arrows can still penetrate and kill a man at full range. A maximum of six of these arrows a minute could be shot from the

Plate 40. Modern replica bodkin arrowhead, made of steel.
By kind permission of Simon Stanley.

bow[6]. The weight of the bow and the force of the arrow were not designed merely to wound or maim opponents. Archery using the war bows was intended to kill. A bodkin arrowhead such as this (Plate 40) is capable of deep penetration and of inflicting serious injury on the major organs, by puncture and incision. Bodkins are also capable of penetrating bone. They were shown to perforate and smash flat bones, but to impact tightly into thick bones, such as vertebrae, from where they proved very difficult to extract[7]. So the war bow, such as those on the *Mary Rose*, was indeed a grim weapon. Its ability to cause instant death was demonstrated both in the French wars and, in England, by battles that took place during the Wars of the Roses. Although battle sites for these wars are known, many burial grounds remain unexplored. An exception is the battle of Towton, which took place in 1461. Here, part of a mass grave was recently excavated and 37 male skeletons were recovered. Examination of their horrific wounds showed the nature of this battle and the following massacre[8]. Many of the wounds had been inflicted by projectiles, probably war bow arrows. The fact that many of these bow men must have known each other, and fought side by side in previous battles against a common enemy, must have added to the horror. In the case of the *Mary Rose* archers, some protection will have been afforded by armour. Not only were there few fractures among the excavated skeletons, but the remains of breastplates, helmets and a small buckler (shield) were found in the hull[9]. Such armour, however, will have provided little protection from heavy arrows with steel armour-piercing heads[6].

When considering the possibility of specialist or professional archers on board, the following points are interesting. First, there is a reference in a contemporary document under "The Army Against France" to:

"archers principals 300, mean archers 200" among other soldiers from the Earl of Arundell's total of "able men 1,272"[10].

This implies that there were some special archers ("principals") in at least one retinue, as well as ordinary ("mean") ones, although we don't know if there were any retinues on board the ship. The idea of specialist bow men does, however, seem to be implied here. Second, a total of 24 bracers (arm guards) were found during the excavation. Twenty-two of these were leather, of which sixteen were decorated in a variety of ways. While some were stamped with a Tudor rose (2) or with flowers (3) two were heraldic, incorporating a pomegranate as part of the design. The pomegranate was the personal emblem of Catherine of Aragon and it is unlikely that such bracers would have been worn by ordinary ("mean") archers[11].

There is reasonable evidence for at least five members of a gun crew from the main deck. Some of these men may have been mariners as well, but the master gunner at least will have had specialist skills. While there is no archaeological evidence for a master gunner in M3 as part of the proposed gun crew, there may be some evidence in M10. Two chests were found in this area close to, but outside, the carpenter's cabin (figure 7). One was in M10 and the other in M9 (figure 10) and each contained, among other things, a linstock and copper alloy priming wire. The one just outside the carpenter's cabin also contained some high-quality personal belongings, including a silver whistle (Call) and some silver jewellery. It has been suggested that these chests belonged to gunners[12]. FCS 89 was found in the same area as the chests. Although without a skull, the skeleton is fairly complete. This man was a little older than many of the others and may, therefore, have been an officer. He was also taller at about 177cm (5' 10") and would have found the conditions on the gun deck cramped. All his bones were strong and robust with very developed muscle attachments. He seems to have used his left arm preferentially, since the bones on this side, particularly those of the lower arm, were bigger and more robust than those on the right. There were many spurs of new bone at attachment sites, including those on the legs and pelvis, and this man appears to have been involved in hard physical work. He may have been a master gunner and the chest containing the Call and jewellery, as well as a linstock and priming wire, may have belonged to him.

Another skeleton associated with particular artefacts is that of FCS 84. This individual was found in M4 in direct association with one of the working Calls. He was also one of the older men, probably in his 30's, and about 163cm (5' 4") tall. He had some back stress and strongly muscled ankles and feet, all of which may have been the result of working in the unstable environment of a ship for most of his life. If the average age of a boatswain was 27, and this man was associated with a working Call, he could have been the boatswain.

FCS 88 was found in O10, in an area of the ship that seems to have contained separate supplies and belongings for the officers[9]. These included some valuable and attractive objects, including the Italian hand guns and gun shields, and also a chest. This chest was of decorated elm and contained clothing and coins. These coins were a large proportion of the total coinage

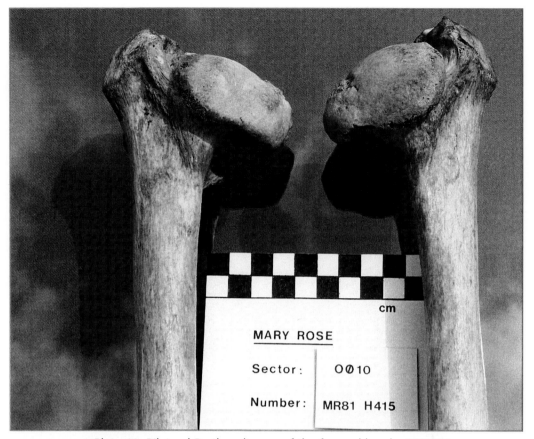

Plate 41. Bilateral Perthes disease of the femoral heads. FCS #88.

found in the hull and consisted of a "mineralised lump" of 45 or more silver coins, plus 7 gold coins[13]. The chest is assumed to have belonged to the purser[12]. FCS 88 was found in the same area of the orlop deck as this chest (figures 10 and 16) and his skeleton is particularly interesting. He was probably in his late twenties or early thirties when he died. What is special about his skeleton is the condition of his hip joints. Both femoral heads are flattened and dropped (Plate 41) and the hip joints are wide and shallow (Plate 42). There is no evidence for a new 'false' hip joint above or near to the normal one, so this is not an example of congenital dislocation of the hip. This man is more likely to have suffered from Perthes disease as a child, the results of which were retained into adult life. Perthes disease is a childhood complaint that affects boys more than girls, particularly between the ages of four and eight. The disease arises when there is an

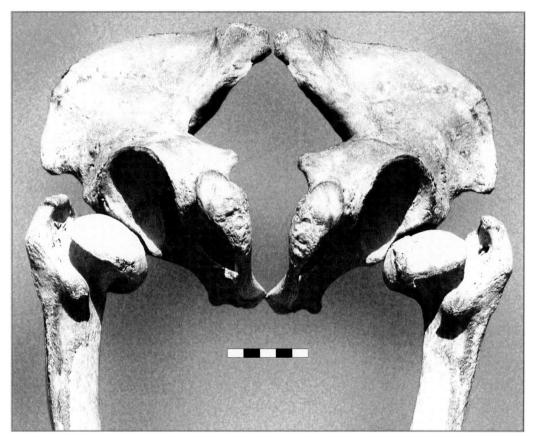

Plate 42. FCS #88: the femurs and their matching hip joints. Bilateral Perthes disease.

osteonecrosis (death of bone) of the head of the femur, perhaps due to trauma[14]. The local blood supply to the bone fails, causing part of it to die, and the femoral head flattens and collapses. The bone heals when the blood supply is restored to the head, but its flat form and the shortening and widening of the femoral neck will still be there in the adult[14]. The condition may lead to osteoarthritis in later life. FCS 88 appears to have had this childhood disease (Plates 41 and 42). The bones have healed and re-formed well, but the initial deformities remain and it is possible that his physical agility was considerably impaired. It was difficult to see what a man with these kinds of disabilities was doing on a warship but, if he had a non-fighting role such as that of the purser, then his physical condition may have been relatively unimportant.

FINAL WORDS

The study of the human skeletal remains from the *Mary Rose* has demonstrated the importance of this kind of work to archaeology. We knew nothing about the men on one of Henry VIII's Great Ships, apart from a few facts about her captain, Roger Grenville and Sir George Carew, the Vice Admiral. However, the examination of the skeletal remains of the crew, and the research conducted on these remains, has given us much information about these men. New techniques are emerging which change our views all the time. For example, Dr. Bell's oxygen isotope work has given us new and valuable information on the origins of some of the men, which supports the documentary record. The work done on the skeleton crew shows the importance of keeping large and unique skeletal collections preserved and available for future study when, no doubt, even more new techniques will become available.

The present work has revealed a group of men who were, in many ways, rather like us in appearance. They were largely young, as one would expect for the crew of a war ship. Their average height was within the range of today's recruits. While many of them may have suffered childhood diseases and, perhaps, starvation, as adults they were mainly strong and robust, with large bones and strong muscles. Much of this was probably as a result of their activities on board the ship. It is reasonable to assume that there was a group of specialist, or professional, archers among these men and it is likely that some of them were regular members of gun crews. It is also feasible that there was a core of professional mariners in the group, since a small number would always be needed as 'shipkeepers'. Some pelvis, leg and foot bones suggest certain individuals had worked in an unstable environment. All of these findings are interesting since, at this time, there are no documentary records for any of them, and no evidence for any professionals in the navy. It is, however, logical that good men whether longbow men, mariners or soldiers would be valuable and used continuously, particularly on such an important vessel.

The British have often been referred to as a seafaring nation and our language is littered with words and phrases which reflect this, such as:

'No room to swing a cat'[15]; 'Above-board' and 'abreast'[16]; To 'get spliced'[17], 'bail out'[18], and 'batten down'[19]; (A clean) 'Bill of Health'[20]; a 'booby'[21].

There are many of these phrases which we use unconsciously and, usually, without thought about their origins. As an island nation, we have a deep emotional attachment to the sea which is never far away, even when we are in the centre of the landmass. Our culture often reflects this attachment, even though many of us are no longer employed on, or in association with, the sea. Marine references, however, exist both in our music and in literature. It is perhaps appropriate to end with the following words from Shakespeare, which must reflect the feelings of the men of the *Mary Rose* on 19th July, 1545:

"Now would I give a thousand furlongs of sea for an acre of barren ground; long heath, brown furze, any thing. The wills above be done! But I would fain die a dry death"[22].

NOTES

1. MRT 3, p 8.
2. Jenny Coy, personal communication, 2000.
3. Frank Green, personal communication, 2000.
4. L. Bell, personal communication, 2000. This work is of great importance to archaeology, since it gives us the opportunity to determine the latitude at birth of the individuals in a burial, providing there are teeth present.
5. Maggie Richards, personal communication, 2000.
6. Simon Stanley, personal communication, 2000.
7. Karger *et al.*, p. 500.
8. Boylston *et al.*, 1997.
9. Alexzandra Hildred, personal communication, 2000.
10. L and P, Vol. 19, Pt. 1, 1544 AD, 273.
11. Letter from W. F. Paterson to the Cdr. Whitlock at the Mary Rose Trust, dated 23rd October,1981.
12. Maggie Richards, personal communication, 2000.
13. Richards, p. 97.
14. Resnick and Niwayama, p. 2875.
15. Oxford Companion to Ships and the Sea, p. 852.
16. *Op. cit.*, p. 3.
17. *Op. cit.*, p. 825.
18. *Op. cit.*, p. 53.
19. *Op. cit.*, p. 65.
20. *Op. cit.*, p. 83.
21. *Op. cit.*, p. 95.
22. William Shakespeare: 'The Tempest' Act I, Scene I, Gonzalo's exit lines.

APPENDIX I

Epiphyses

THE EPIPHYSES

The epiphyses include the growth plates of the skeleton. They are situated at the ends of the long bones of the limbs, the short bones of the hands and feet and at the edges of the flat bones of the pelvis and

Plate 43. An immature humerus with a loose epiphysis (right). A fully mature humerus with a fused epiphysis is shown on the left.

the scapula (figure 12). The epiphyses are part of the articular joint surfaces in the long and short bones (Plate 43), and are attached to the main part of the bones by a thin layer of cartilage, thus allowing the bones to continue growth. The epiphyses fuse to the main bone when skeletal maturity is achieved and growth stops.

APPENDIX II

Stature and Various Skeletal Indices

Stature

The Trotter American 'White Male' formula applied to the femur for the calculation of stature is:

($2.38 \times$ maximum length of the femur in cm $+ 61.41$) $+/- 3.27$cm [Trotter, 1970].

This gives a height in centimeters with a Standard Deviation of 3.27cm, which can then be converted, if necessary, to inches by dividing the result by a factor of 2.54. The results are shown in Table 1. Actual, living height will be a little more than skeletal height because of the connective and other tissue present in the living body but not in the skeleton, and a small adjustment has to be made to the formula when estimating the height of

Table 1: Stature based on the femur

Left femur	Right femur	Combined FCS femurs
N = 82	N = 92	N = 104
X = 170.9	X = 171.2	X = 170.6
SD = 4.5	SD = 5.0	SD = 4.6
(5' 7" +/- 1.8")	(5' 7.5" +/- 2")	(5' 7" +/- 1.8")

Key: measurements in cm: N = number; X = mean; SD = standard deviation.

older individuals. There were 82 left femora and 92 right femora which were measurable from across the ship. Mean stature was calculated from both left and right femora and also from the combined left and right values for the FCS group.

The results from both sides and from using the combined FCS bones are the same.

The Cranial Index

The Cranial Index is derived in the following way, using a vernier caliper to take the relevant measurements [Bass, 1971: 54–69]:

Cranial Index:

$$\frac{\text{Maximum Cranial breadth} \times 100}{\text{Maximum Cranial length}}$$

Traditionally, four categories have been used to express the results:

Dolichocranic = X*- 74.9 – narrow or long headed
Mesocranic = 75.0 – 79.9 – average or medium headed
Brachycranic = 80.0 – 84.9 – broad or round headed
Hyperbrachycranic = 85.0 – X* – very broad headed
*where X is an unknown figure

A total of 99 skulls were in a suitable condition to provide all the necessary measurements for the derivation of the Cranial Index and the results were as follows:

Table 2: Cranial Index

Category	Number of crania
X *– 74.9	44
75.0 – 79.9	44
80.0 – 84.9	10
85.0 – X*	1
TOTAL	99

*where X is an unknown figure

Although the majority of the values were clustered together in the first two groups, it was unclear how they were distributed within these groups, and the actual measurements ranged from 67.5–90.0. This suggested that there might be further sub-groups within the usual ranges. Therefore, new categories were devised to see if the larger clusters could be refined. They were:

Table 3: 'New' Cranial Index

Category	Number of crania
67.5 – 69.9	4
70.0 – 72.4	9
72.5 – 74.9	31
75.0 – 77.4	25
77.5 – 79.9	19
80.0 – 82.4	9
82.5 – 84.9	1
85.0 – 87.4	1
TOTAL	99

Using this method, the largest single cluster falls within a subgroup in the dolichocranic range.

The Orbital Index

The Orbital Index is derived in the following way [Bass, op.cit.]:

$$\text{Orbital Index:} \quad \frac{\text{Maximum Orbital height} \times 100}{\text{Maximum Orbital breadth}}$$

Three categories are traditionally used to express the results:

Chamaeconchy = X* – 82.9 – wide orbits
Mesoconchy = 83.0 – 89.9 – average or medium orbits
Hypsiconchy = 89.0 – X* – narrow orbits
*where X is an unknown figure

A total of 85 skulls could be measured for this index and the results were:

Table 4: Orbital Index

Categories	Number of individuals
X* – 82.9	32
83.0 – 89.9	33
90.0 – *X	20
TOTAL	85

*where X is an unknown figure

A similar clustering occurred to that for the Cranial Index, with the majority of measurements in the first two categories: the range was from 72.5 – 120. Again, it was unclear how the measurements were distributed within the broad categories and whether there were sub-groups within the broad ranges. Accordingly, new categories were devised, to see if the large clusters could be refined. They were:

Table 5: 'New' Orbital Index

Categories	Number of individuals
72.5 – 75.9	5
76.0 – 79.4	9
79.5 – 82.9	18
83.0 – 86.4	14
86.5 – 89.9	19
90.0 – 93.4	6
93.5 – 96.9	6
97.0 – 100.4	5
100.5 – 103.9	2
104.0 – 107.4	1
TOTAL	85

Using this method, the largest cluster falls within a subgroup in the mesoconchy range.

The Total Facial Index

The Total Facial Index is derived from two measurements [Bass, op. cit.]:

Total Facial Index $\quad\quad\dfrac{\text{Total facial height} \times 100}{\text{Bizygomatic breadth}}$

where total facial height measures the whole face from nasion (the nasal bridge) to gnathion (the point of the chin) and bizygomatic breadth is the greatest distance between the zygomatic arches (cheek bones).

The derivation of this index is dependant on both the skull and the mandible surviving in a good enough condition for the necessary measurements to be taken. Five categories are used to express the results:

Hypereuryprosopy = X^* – 79.9 – very broad face
Euryprosopy = 80.0 – 84.9 – broad face
Mesoprosopy = 85.0 – 89.9 – average or medium face
Leptoprosopy = 90.0 – 94.9 – slender or narrow face
Hyperleptoprosopy = 95.0 – X^* – very narrow face
*where X is an unknown figure

A total of 50 matched skulls and mandibles were in a suitable condition for the relevant measurements to be taken and the results were:

Table 6: Total Facial Index

Categories	Number of individuals
X^* – 79.9	6
80.0 – 84.9	13
85.0 – 89.9	12
90.0 – 94.9	12
95.0 – X^*	7

*where X is an unknown figure

These results show an even spread of face shapes between the broad, average and narrow face ranges.

The normal form of the distributions for all the above indices make it likely that the heads of the whole crew were probably similar in shape and form to those that have been measured. Therefore, it is statistically unlikely that the distribution would be skewed in one direction or another by the addition of the remainder of the group.

Post-cranial Indices

The robusticity index expresses the relative size of the shafts of either the humerus or the femur. It is derived by making calculations based on specific measurements of the shaft of the bone. For the humerus these are [Bass, op. cit. p 115]:

$$\text{Robusticity Index:} \quad \frac{\text{Minimum circumference of the shaft} \times 100}{\text{Maximum length of the humerus}}$$

For the femur they are [Bass, op. cit., p 170]:

$$\text{Robusticity Index:} \quad \frac{\text{Diameter of the shaft at mid-point} \times 100}{\text{Bicondylar length}}$$

Note: The diameter of the shaft of the femur at mid-point is derived by measuring, with calipers, the anterior-posterior and medio-lateral diameters of the shaft. The bicondylar length is different from the maximum length of the bone, being measured with the distal condyles of the knee joint flat against the osteometric board and the head at the other end. All measurements must be taken with great care and at the same points on every bone. In this way, they can be repeated from bone to bone and by different workers with a reasonable degree of accuracy.

APPENDIX III

Femoral Angles and Attachments

Femoral angles

The angle at which the head and neck of the femur meet the shaft is variable. This angle was measured on X-rays and compared for the two groups. The results showed that the *Mary Rose* men had a lower value for this angle than the men from Norwich. The crew also had stronger negative correlations between the angle and the midshaft transverse diameter of their femora than did the Norwich men. It has been argued that a negative correlation between these two dimensions suggests high levels of activity and mechanical stress at the hip [Trinkhaus, p 294]. If we accept this argument, it follows that the ship's crew was probably involved in higher levels of activity and physical stress than the men from Norwich. Of course, we cannot specify which particular activity may have caused the stresses, but this evidence would support that from the muscle attachment sites.

Muscle attachments

Muscles attach to bone in two areas. Formerly, these areas were known as the origin and the insertion of a muscle and it was thought that the origin of the muscle was static, while the insertion moved. However, these terms are now considered to be rather rigid, since the part of the muscle that moves is dependent both on the muscle and on its action [L. Scheuer, personal communication]. It is more acceptable these days to speak of the attachments of muscle to bone as either the proximal and distal or the medial and lateral attachment, depending on the muscle.

There are areas of the pelvis where certain muscles attach, which also show signs of stress in young men from the crew. This applies in particular to the pubis, where the large muscles that adduct the thigh attach proximally. These muscles are also involved, with others such as the hamstrings, in flexion and extension of the hip and the thigh. While they attach on the pubic area of the pelvis, these muscles also attach distally on the posterior of the femur, forming a large fan [Kapandji, Vol.2 p 59, and figure 137]. Out of a total of 19 men who have such changes in the FCS group, 9 belong to young individuals, of whom 5 have signs of muscle stress on the pubis. We have seen that many femora in this group have extremely well developed muscle attachment sites on the posterior femur, as elsewhere (Plate 4). The development of these sites suggests an increased use of the adductors, the flexors and the extensors of the hips and thigh. A similar development of the attachment sites of these muscles on the pubis supports this view.

The thigh muscles that attach on the pelvis can also be used in flexion and extension of the hip and thigh, as well as in their primary role as adductors. When the body is supported on both limbs, the adductors are used to stabilise the pelvis. They are also essential in maintaining certain postures in some sports [Kapandji, p 61, figure 142]. They are used by a longbow archer when at full draw and shooting at a 45° angle (Plates 33 and 34). Their increased size in some of the *Mary Rose* crew supports the idea of the presence of a group of young men using a heavy war bow.

Abbreviations

L and P: *Letters and Papers, Foreign and Domestic of the reign of King Henry VIII.*
MM: *Mariner's Mirror.*
MRT, 3: Mary Rose Trust, 3, 1997.
Opp: Oppenheim.
R.O: Record Office

Glossary

abduction: movement of a limb or part of the body away from the central axis.

adduction: movement of a limb or part of the body towards the central axis.

anaerobic: an environment in which there is no free oxygen from the air.

arquebus: an early portable gun which was supported on a forked rest or tripod.

bilateral symmetry: two sides equally balanced about a plane.

bonaventure mizzen: the farthest aft mast of a sailing ship. In the 16th century the bonaventure was the fourth farthest mast aft.

cannon: a short, stubby gun, firing heavy iron shot.

carrack: a 15th and 16th century large ocean-going merchant ship, with high fore and after castles.

carvel build: a method of wooden ship building, where edge-to-edge planking is laid over a timber frame.

caulking: a method of making a ship's seams watertight, using old rope fibres ('oakum') and pitch.

clinker build: a method of wooden ship building, where the ship is built up from the keel with overlapping planks which are later strengthened by adding light frames.

cortex; cortical: (of bone), the compact bone lying close to the bone surface.

culverin: a large, muzzle-loading gun, longer and thinner than a cannon, and firing lighter shot to a greater distance.

curtall: a large bronze gun, possibly the pre-cursor to the cannon. It fired 18kg (40lb) shot and was last inventoried in 1523.

demesne: land held by the lord of the manor for his own use. Part of the main manor farm, the unfree tenants (villeins) had to work this land without pay in exchange for their own living.

demi-cannon: a gun of the cannon type but firing lighter shot than a cannon.

demi-culverin: a culverin type gun, firing a shot of about 4kg (9lb).

distal: furthest away from the point of origin or the mid-line. In the body, furthest away from the head.

eburnation: bone-on-bone polishing at a joint, when all the cartilage lining the opposing surfaces has disintegrated.

enthesophytes; enthesopathies: bony outgrowths (osteophytes) at the sites of tendon or ligament attachments on bone.

epiphyses: the areas of immature bone where growth (increase in size) takes place.

falcon: a small, muzzle-loading bronze gun of the culverin class.

frames: the ship's skeleton, composed of the keel and pairs of timbers to support her sides.

furlong: originally, the length of a furrow in an open field, or a rectangular block of strips, 200m (220yd) in linear measurement.

galleass: a 16th century oared sailing warship.

galley: a warship which was rowed. Also, the kitchen of a ship, down in the hold in the case of the *Mary Rose*.

keel: the spine of a ship, running along the centre of the bottom of the hull.

knee: the large 'ribs' of a ship, shaped like a knee with an angular bend.

lade; lading: to put cargo on board a ship.

lateral: away from the mid-line (of the body).

linstock: a short wooden staff, used to fire a gun. It had a slow-burning match held at one end. Many linstocks from the *Mary Rose* were individually carved.

medial: towards the mid-line (of the body).

morrispikes: a form of pike, supposedly of Moorish origin.

murderer: a small, breech-loading gun, probably firing small pieces of metal either loose or in canisters. These guns changed their form over time.

osteonecrosis: the pathological death of some bone cells.

osteophytes: outgrowths of new bone around the margins of a joint.

periosteum: a fibrous membrane covering the surfaces of bone, apart from the joints.

pike: the forerunner of the bayonet. A long wooden staff with a pointed iron or steel head.

pleura; pleural: the membrane surrounding the lungs and lining the chest cavity; pertaining to the lungs.

primogeniture: the first-born child. The system in the feudal state whereby the eldest son inherited all his father's estate in the case of intestacy.

proximal: closest to the point of origin or midline. In the body, closest to the head.

purveyance: the historical right of the sovereign to supply provisions at a fixed price.

retinue: a body of retainers, belonging to an important personage.

rider: an extra beam placed internally over the planking of a ship's hold.

rowbarge: a type of 16th century small oared warship.

seignory: a lord's land holding, usually a manor.

selion: the cultivated strip in the open medieval field, it was ploughed to form a ridge with furrows at either side for drainage.

seneschal: the steward who overlooked and ran all the lord's manors.

serpentine: an early, light breech-loading gun.

socage: free tenure without the obligation of military service to the lord; abolished in 1660.

stringer: a longitudinal wooden beam, part of the structure of a ship's hull.

vascular channels: longitudinal marks on bone, left by the impression of the blood vessels which lay there.

yard: a large diagonal or horizontal spar, which crosses the mast and supports a sail.

Bibliography

Adams, J. Crawford, *Outline of Orthopaedics.* Ninth Edition. Churchill Livingstone, 1981.

——, *Outline of Fractures.* Seventh Edition. Churchill Livingstone, 1978, reprinted 1982.

Aiello, L and Dean, C., *An Introduction to Human Evolutionary Anatomy.* Academic Press, 1990.

Anderson, R.C., Armaments in 1540. *Mariners Mirror*, 6, 1920; p. 281.

Andrews, K.R., *The Elizabethan Seaman.* National Maritime Museum, 1982: pp. 245–63.

Annals of the Barber Surgeons of London. By Sidney Young. Blades, East and Blades, 1890

Baker, Richard, Shipshape for Discoveries, and Return. *Mariners Mirror*, 78, 1992.

Bartlett, Clive and Embleton, Gerry, *English Longbowman 1330–1515.* Osprey Military Warrior Series No.11, 1995.

Bass, William, M., *Human Osteology: A Laboratory and Field Guide of the Human Skeleton.* 2nd edition. Special Publication of the Missouri Archaeological Society, 1971.

Bird, H., *When the body takes the strain.* New Scientist, 7 July, 1990.

Boylston, A. Novak, S. Sutherland, T. Holst, M. and Coughlan, J., *Burials from the Battle of Towton.* Royal Armouries Yearbook, 2, pp. 36–9, 1997.

Brigden, Susan, *New Worlds, Lost Worlds; the Rule of the Tudors 1485–1603.* Penguin Books 2001.

M.de Brossard, The French and English versions of the loss of the *Mary Rose* in 1545. *Mariners Mirror*, 70, p. 387, 1984.

Brothwell, D. R., *Digging Up Bones.* BMNH, 1981.

Bruce, M.S. Campbell, *The population of early Tudor England: a re-evaluation of the 1522 Muster Returns and 1524 and 1525 Lay Subsidies.* Journal of Historical Geography, 7:2, pp. 145–54, 1981.

Coates, J.F., *Flower of the Fleet*. The Naval Architect, June 1985.

Copies of Transcripts and Extracts from Wills and other Records Collected by Miss Olive Moger *c*. 1921–1941, Vol. III (Bremel-Cawley). West Country Studies Library, Exeter.

Corbett, M.E. and Anderson, R.J., *Dental Caries in the Crew of a Tudor Warship*. Journal of Dental Research, 69, 968. Abstract 112. 1990.

Cornwall, Julian, *English Population in the Early Sixteenth Century*. Economic History Review, second series. XXIII, 1: 32–44, 1970.

Davies, C.S.L., *The Administration of the Royal Navy under Henry VIII: the origins of the Navy Board*. English Historical Review, 1965: 268–288. 1980.

——, *Provisions for Armies, 1509–50; A Study in the Effectiveness of Early Tudor Government*. Economic History Review, Second Series, 15; 2: 234–248, 1964.

Dymond, David, *The Famine of 1527 in Essex*. Local Population Studies, no 26, Spring 1981.

Entick, John, *A New Naval History*, London 1757.

Floud, R., Wachter, K. and Gregory, A., *Height, health and history: Nutritional Status in the UK 1750–1980*. Cambridge Studies in Population, Economy and Society in Past Times. CUP, 1990.

Fraser, Antonia, *The Six Wives of Henry VIII*, Mandarin, 1992.

Goodman, W. W., Bristol Apprentice Register, 1532–1658: a selection of enrolments of mariners. *Mariners Mirror*, 60; 27–31, 1974.

Gosse, P, *Sea Surgeons*. Edinburgh Review: 237; 319–330. 1923.

Grant, Alison, *Grenville*, North Devon Museum Trust, 1991.

Gray's Anatomy, Descriptive and Applied. 32nd Edition. Edited by T. B. Johnston, D. V. Davies and F. Davies. Longmans, Green and Co. Ltd. 1958.

Hannay, David, *A Short History of the Royal Navy 1217–1688*. Methuen, 1898.

Hair, P.E.H., and J.D. Alsop, *English Seamen and Traders in Guinea 1553–1565: The New Evidence of Their Wills*. Studies in British History, Vol. 31. Edwin Mellen Press, 1992.

Hardy, Robert, *Longbow: a Social and Military History*. Patrick Stephens Ltd., Sparkford, Somerset, 1995.

Harrison, G.A., Tanner, J.M., Pilbeam, D.R. and Baker, P.T., *Human Biology: an Introduction to Human Evolution, Variation, Growth and Adaptability*. 3rd Edition, Oxford Science Publications, 1988.

Hildred, Alexzandra, *The Material Culture of the Mary Rose as a fighting vessel: the uses of wood*. Oxbow Monograph 84, 1997.

Hoskins, W. G., Harvest and Hunger. *The Listener*, December 10 1964.

Howard, G. F., Gun Port Lids. *Mariners Mirror*; 67, p. 64, 1981.

Işcan, M. Y., Loth, S. R. and Wright, R. K., *Age Estimation from the Rib by Phase Analysis: White Males*. Journal of Forensic Sciences, Vol. 29, number 4, October 1984.

Kapandji, I.A., *The Physiology of the Joints: Annotated Diagrams of the Mechanics of the Human Joints*, Vol.2, Lower Limb. 2nd Edition, Churchill Livingstone, 1983.

Karger, B., Sudhues, H., Kneubuehl, B.P. and Brinkmann, B., *Experimental Arrow Wounds: Ballistics and Traumatology*. The Journal of Trauma: Injury, Infection and Critical Care, 45 (3), 495–501. 1998.

Keevil, J.J., *Medicine and the Navy 1200–1900*. Vol. 1: 1200–1649. Livingstone, London 1957.

Kemp, *The British Sailor*. Dent, London, 1970.

Krogman, W. M., *The Human Skeleton in Forensic Medicine*. Charles C. Thomas, Springfield, 1978.

Kunitz, Stephen J., *Making a Long Story Short: a Note on Men's Height and Mortality in England from the First through the 19th Centuries*. Medical History, 31: 269–280, 1987.

Letters and Papers, Foreign and Domestic of the Reign of Henry VIII. Arranged and Catalogued by J. Gairdner and R. H. Brodie. *HMSO*, 1905 and 1920.

Liberson, F., *Os acromiale – a contested anomaly. Journal of Bone and Joint Surgery*, Vol. 19: 683–89, 1937.

Livi-Bacci, Massimo, *Population and Nutrition: An Essay on European Demographic History*. Cambridge Studies in Population, Economy and Society in Past Time. Cambridge University Press, 1991.

Loades, David, *The Tudor Navy: An administrative, political and military history*. Studies in Naval History. General Editor, N.A.M. Rodger. Scolar Press, 1992.

Maat, G.J.R., *Scurvy in Dutch Whalers buried at Spitzbergen*. Proceedings of the 4th European Meeting of the Paleopathology Association, Middleburg: 82–93, 1982.

Mann, D.L., and Littke, N., *Shoulder Injuries in Archery*. Canadian Journal of Sports Science, Vol. 14, Pt. 2: 85–92, 1989.

McKee, Alexander., Notes: the *Mary Rose*'s Complement. *Mariners Mirror*, 72; 74, 1986.

McMinn, R.M.H. and Hutchings, R.T., *A Colour Atlas of Human Anatomy*. Wolfe Medical Publications, London, 1985.

Mensforth, R.P., Lovejoy, C.O., Lallo, J.W., and Armelagos, G.J., *The Role of Constitutional Factors, Diet and Infectious Disease in the Etiology of Porotic Hyperostosis and Periosteal Reactions in Prehistoric Infants and Children.* Medical Anthropology, Vol.2, issue 1; 1–59, 1978.

Merbs, Charles. F., *Patterns of Activity-Induced Pathology in a Canadian Inuit Population.* Archaeological Survey of Canada, Paper No. 119. National Museums of Canada, 1983.

Miles, A.E.W., *The Dentition in the Assessment of Individual Age in Skeletal Material.* Dental Anthropology, London, 1963.

——, *Non-union of the Epiphysis of the Acromion in the Skeletal Remains of a Scottish Population of c. 1700.* International Journal of Osteoarchaeology, Vol. 4: 149–163, 1994.

Molleson, T. and Cox, M., *The Spitalfields Project, Vol. 2 – The Anthropology: The Middling Sort.* CBA Research Report no. 86, York, 1993.

Nicholson, G.P., Goodman, D.A., Flatow, E.L., and Bigliani L.U., *The acromion: morphologic condition and age-related changes. A study of 420 scapulas.* Journal of Shoulder and Elbow Surgery, Vol. 5 (1): 1-11, 1996 (Abstract).

Oppenheim, M., *A History of the Administration of the Royal Navy and of Merchant Shipping in relation to the Navy.* Vol 1, pp. 45–99, London 1896. [NB: Rodger says that, although extensively used, it is important to understand that Oppenheim was extremely prejudiced against Royal government and that his figures, quotations and references are very untrustworthy.]

Ortner, D.J. and Putschar, W.G.J., *Identification of Pathological Conditions in Human Skeletal Remains.* Smithsonian Contributions to Anthropology number 28. 1985.

Ortner, D.J. and Eriksen, M.F., *Bone Changes in the Human Skull Probably Resulting from Scurvy in Infancy and Childhood.* International Journal of Osteoarchaeology Vol. 7; 212–220 1997.

Ortner, D.J., Kimmerle, E.H. and Diez, M., *Probable Evidence of Scurvy in Subadults from Archaeolgical Sites in Peru.* AJPA 108: 321–331, 1999.

Oxford Companion to Ships and the Sea. Edited by Peter Kemp. Oxford University Press, 1988.

Pratt, Professor P.L., *Testing the Bows*, in Hardy, Robert: *Longbow*, 1995.

Prynne, M.W., *Mariners Mirror*, 54, 123, 1968.

Public records of the blitzing of Exeter in May, 1942. West Country Studies Library, Exeter.

Rees, Gareth, The longbow's deadly secrets. In *New Scientist*, pp. 24-25, 5th June, 1993.

Resnick, Donald and Niwayama, Gen., *Diagnosis of Bone and Joint Disorders*. W. B. Saunders, Philadelphia, 1981.

Richards, Maggie, *Form, function, ownership: a study of chests from Henry VIII's warship* Mary Rose (1545). Oxbow Monograph 84; pp. 87–98, 1997.

Richardson, John, *The Local Historian's Encyclopaedia*. Historical Publications, 1989.

Roberts, C. and Manchester, K., *The Archaeology of Disease*. 2nd Edition. Sutton, Stroud, 1995.

Rodger, N.A.M., *The Safeguard of the Sea: A Naval History of Britain*, Volume One: 660–1649. HarperCollins and the National Maritime Museum. 1997.

Rogers, Juliet and Waldron, Tony, *A Field Guide to Joint Disease in Archaeology*. John Wiley and Sons, 1995.

Rowse, A.L., *Tudor Cornwall*. Dyllansow Truan, Redruty. 1991.

Rule, M., *The Mary Rose*. Windward Press, 1982.

Scammel, G.V., *War at Sea under the Early Tudors: the Newcastle upon Tyne evidence*. Archaeologia Aeliana, 4th series; vol 39; 179–205. 1961.

——, *Shipowning in England*. Transactions of the Royal History Society, 5th series; Vol 12, 1962.

——, Manning the English Merchant Service in the Sixteenth Century. *Mariners Mirror* LVI, pp. 131–54, 1970.

Sharman, I.M., *Vitamin requirements of the human body*. In *Starving Sailors*, ed. by J. Watt, E.J. Freeman and W. F. Bynum. National Maritime Museum 1981.

Slack, Paul, *The Impact of Plague in Tudor and Stuart England*. Clarendon, Oxford, 1990.

Spont, A., *Letters and Papers Relating to the War with France 1512–1514*. Navy Records Society, 10. 1897–98.

Steinbock, R. Ted., *Paleopathological Diagnosis and Interpretation: bone diseases in ancient human populations*. Charles C. Thomas, Springfield, 1976.

Sterling, J.C., Meyers, M.C., Chesshir, W., and Calvo, R.D., *Os acromiale in a Baseball Catcher*. Medicine and Science in Sports and Exercise, Vol. 27 (6): 795–9, 1995 (Abstract).

Stirland, Ann, *A Possible Correlation between Os acromiale and Occupation in the Burials from the* Mary Rose. Proceedings of the Fifth European Meeting of the Paleopathology Association, Siena: 327–334, 1984.

Stirland, A.J., *Asymmetry and Activity-Related Change in Selected Bones of the Human Male Skeleton.* PhD Thesis, University College London, 1992

Stirland, A.J., *Asymmetry and Activity-related Change in the Male Humerus.* International Journal of Osteoarchaeology, Vol. 3: 105–113, 1993.

Stirland, Ann., *Human Bones in Archaeology,* Second edition. Shire Archaeology, 1999.

Stirland, A.J. and Waldron, T., *Evidence for Activity Related Markers in the Vertebrae of the Crew of the* Mary Rose. Journal of Archaeological Science, 24, 329–335. 1997.

Stone, A.C., Milner, G.R., Paabo, S and Stonking, M., *Sex determination of ancient skeletons using DNA.* American Journal of Physical Anthropology, 99, 231–8, 1996.

Suchey, J.M. and Brooks, S.T., *Skeletal Age Determination based on the Male Os Pubis.* Presentation, 12th International Congress of Anthropological and Ethnological Sciences, Zagreb, 1988, and accompanying casts.

Taylor, Geoffrey. *Clinical Manifestations of Vitamin Deficiencies.* In *Starving Sailors,* ed. by J.Watt, E. J. Freeman and W. F. Bynum. National Maritime Museum, 1981.

The *Mary Rose*: Exhibition and Ship Hall. The Mary Rose Trust 3, 1997.

Tiller, Kate, *English Local History: an Introduction.* Sutton, Stroud. 1992.

Trevelyan, G.M., *English Social History: A Survey of Six Centuries – Chaucer to Queen Victoria.* Longmans, Green and Co. 1947.

Trinkhaus, E., *The evolution of the Hominid femoral diaphysis during the Upper Pleistocene in Europe and the Near East.* Z. Morph. Anthrop., vol 67, no 3; 291–319. Stuttgart, 1976.

Trotter, M., *Estimation of Stature from Intact Long Limb Bones.* In *Personal Identification in Mass Disasters.* Ed. T. D. Stewart. Smithsonian Institution, Washington D.C., 1970.

Ubelaker, D.H., *Human Skeletal Remains: Excavation, Analysis, Interpretation.* Taraxacum, Washington D.C., 1984.

Vice-Admiral Sir Henry Kitson, The Early History of Portsmouth Dockyard, 1496–1800. *Mariners Mirror,* 33, 1947.

Visitation of Buckinghamshire in 1634: Additional Pedigrees p. 203. Publications of the Harleian Society, Vol. LVIII; MDCCCCIX (1909).

Wakely, Jennifer, Manchester, Keith and Roberts, Charlotte, *Scanning Electron Microscopy of Rib Lesions.* International Journal of Osteoarchaeology, 1, 185–189. 1991.

Watt, Sir James, *Some Consequences of Nutritional Disorders in*

Eighteenth-Century British Circumnavigations. In *Starving Sailors*, ed. by J. Watt, E.J. Freeman and W. F. Bynum. National Maritime Museum, 1981.

Watt, James, Surgeons of the Mary Rose: the practise of surgery in Tudor England. *Mariners Mirror*, 69: 3–19, 1983.

Waldron, Tony, *Counting the Dead. The Epidemiology of Skeletal Populations.* John Wiley and Sons Ltd., Chichester, 1994.

Waldron, T., *A Note on the Estimation of Height from Long Bone Measurements.* International Journal of Osteoarchaeology, Vol. 8:1: 75–77, 1998.

Whitlock, Peter, The Boatswain's Call: an updating. *Mariners Mirror*, 71: 167–168. 1985.

Wood, A.B., The Lord Admiral's Whistle: quotes from the life of Sir Peter Carewe in *Archaeologia*, vol 28, about the appointment of Sir George Carewe to be "Vyce Admyrall of that journey, and had apoynted unto hyme a shippe named the Marye Rose"; the King giving his own whistle and chain is also in this passage. *Mariners Mirror*, 5, 1919: 58.

Youings, Joyce, *Sixteenth Century England. The Pelican Social History of England*, Penguin 1988.

Youings, Joyce and Cornford, Peter W., *Seafaring and Maritime Trade in Sixteenth Century Devon.* In the *New Maritime History of Devon*, 1. Conway Maritime Press in association with the University of Exeter. 1992.

Index

Page numbers in *italic* relate to figures, plates and tables.